THROUGH MY EYES

A Look at the History of Lancaster from a Black Perspective

Hollie Ann Saunders

in the spirit of excellence

Reynoldsburg, Ohio

Published in association with Ambassador Press, LLC
PO Box 722
Reynoldsburg, OH 43068
www.ambassadorpressllc.com

Copyright ©2007 Hollie Ann Saunders
Cover design by Marcia Rose

First Ambassador Press, LLC printing, September 2007

ISBN 0-9787850-1-0

Dedication

This book is dedicated to those who were supportive and an encouragement to me during the long process of putting this book together.

First of all, I give praise, glory and honor to my Lord, Jesus Christ for giving me the ability and means to write this book. I thank Him for sustaining the black community, for we know that "we have come this far by faith."

I want to thank my parents, Alice and Ken Saunders, and the rest of my family, not only for the information they related to me but for helping me and feeding me during the low points.

I am grateful to my daughter, Heather Noel, for her patience and understanding, and for letting me on the computer for hours at a time, especially when she wanted to be online. My faithful "sidekick," Chloe, stayed at my feet or on the nearby bed, keeping me company and listening to me when I read passages out loud.

A special thank you to Lorraine Arnold and Marty Lebold for their friendly "threats" if I did not complete this book. Thanks, I was dragging my feet, and you both helped me over the hump to finish. I am so appreciative to Marcia Rose for all her help, support, and suggestions. Thanks also go to my friend, Mary Holt, for looking at my draft with a professional eye. Also thanks to my online friend from Chicagoland, Scott, who helped restore my enthusiasm when I was at a low point in my life. Geno, thank you for your love and support, for being you, and helping me to remember to "keep it real and handle my business!"

Aunt Dolores, I finally did it!! We did it!! Thank you for the box that helped me to finish this book. I am so glad that you were diligent in keeping articles, information and notes throughout your lifetime. I felt your presence most of the time while I was typing.

Introduction

When I was a little girl, I liked to sit near the adults and listen to the stories of their lives, about the older people in town, and whatever was going on within the black community of Lancaster, Ohio, a small town about 30 miles from Columbus, the State Capital. In 1983, the editor of the *Lancaster Eagle-Gazette* asked me if I would write a series of articles for Black History Month. I always had a secret dream to write for our local newspaper, so I agreed. I went to the Fairfield County District Library to research any documented history of the black community in the number of books written about the history of Lancaster and Fairfield County. I was a little surprised and more disappointed that there was virtually nothing written, except for several lines about one or two prominent black citizens and about Allen Chapel A.M.E. Church, the historical black church located on Walnut Street.

Writing several articles for one month proved to be quite a challenge. I went to my family and friends, and church records to write the articles, however, and I continued to write articles during Black History Month for several years. Each time, I relied on the stories I remembered from my youth and the stories passed down to other black residents. At one point, I talked with local white residents as to their perception and memories of the black community.

During this time, Dolores Carlisle, her sister-in-law, Joan Carlisle, and I began to interview people and record their experiences as one of the objectives for the Black Interest Group. We thought it would be important to make sure the information we gathered was kept safe for us and for the future generations, black or white.

The feedback from the articles I wrote was very positive. Several people encouraged me to take it a step further and to put the information and stories in a book. After some thought and consideration, and talks with Aunt Dolores, we thought it would be a good idea to write a book. What better way to let people know that there has always been a viable community of black people who made significant contributions to the city of Lancaster. We believe our history is important for all people to be aware of, and that the previously written books on the history of Lancaster and Fairfield County were incomplete because they did not include the black families who lived and worked here.

There are so many stories and experiences that I did not include all of them in this particular book. I wanted to focus more on the overall history of the black community and on people who were and are familiar to those who live in Lancaster. This is almost all based on the oral histories gathered and stories I heard, as well as information I gathered from other people in town.

It is my hope that, as they read this book, people will be able to identify with the topics mentioned and recall memories of their own. Even if any readers are not familiar with any of the people or events mentioned, to me, it is important for people to know that the one percent of the city's population who are black, indeed lived here and were, and still are, an integral part of Lancaster.

Chapter One

Coming to the New Frontier

Lancaster, Ohio. My hometown.

I love it, and I am proud to say this is where I grew up and still live.

Lancaster, a town with a population of almost 37,000 people, and is nestled in the hills on the edge of central Ohio or southeastern Ohio, whichever it wants to claim. Coming from Columbus to the north, you leave the flatlands to enter the rolling hills of the Hocking Hills region to the south. We have rich, fertile farmlands in and surrounding Lancaster in Fairfield County. We boast of being a state Tree City, which adds to the beauty of the area. Many parks are scattered around town for families and individuals to enjoy, including the two biggest parks--Alley Park to the south and Rising Park located in town at the base of our famous landmark, Mount Pleasant. No matter how many times I drive in and out of Lancaster, I still catch my breath and marvel at the natural beauty of my hometown.

My dad, Ken Saunders, was born and raised in Lancaster, and my mom, Alice Saunders, grew up in Hocking County. She told me when she first came to Lancaster with her sister and other relatives, she was amazed at how clean and pretty the town was, and how friendly most of the people were. She said she used to tell herself she would not mind living in Lancaster when she grew older. Little did she know that she would meet my dad, marry him, and move here to raise their children.

Lancaster is not perfect--all cities, towns, and villages have their problems. But, to me, it is better than most places I've been. The only real complaint I have, with which some people might disagree, is the rapid changes that have taken place in recent years. As our small town shows signs of growing into a sprawling city, it is my fear that the historical roots of Lancaster will not reach deep enough and become grounded with those who move here.

As a result of this growth spurt, Lancaster is becoming a busy city with constant building of new developments and home subdivisions. The boundaries are reaching further out in all directions as people from all over fall in love with our beautiful corner of Fairfield County and decide to settle down. This is not much different than what must have taken place in the very early years of the 1800s.

Rising Park is one of my favorite places to go. Mom and Dad often took us there on a Sunday afternoon. While we played on the play equipment, Mom sat and watched us, and Dad played horseshoes with his cousins and friends, including Stanley Carlisle and Sam Nichols. When I was in high school, a lot of us teens used to go out there to cruise and show off our cars, wash our cars near the upper shelter house, ice skate in the winter, or, in warm weather, sit and enjoy the weather or each other's company. After I graduated, I often took a book and spent peaceful times on top of Mount Pleasant, looking down on Lancaster. From there, I was able to look out over the horizon for miles and miles. I used to imagine this is what the Indians who lived in the area did when the first settlers began to arrive. I think they were worried and upset about the changes they would experience, as the number of settlers increased.

In 1797, during the presidency of John Adams, Ebenezer Zane was contracted by the United States government to open a road from Wheeling, West Virginia to Limestone, now Maysville, Kentucky. The country at that time was an unbroken wilderness the entire distance of 226 miles. He successfully accomplished the work and the route was named Zane's Trace.

As part of his compensation for blazing Zane's Trace, Ebenezer received tracts of land, patented to him by Congress. One of these tracts was located where Zanesville now stands, and one embraced the present site of Lancaster.

In the fall of 1800, Zane laid out and sold the first lots in Lancaster. To encourage emigration to the area, Zane gave a few lots in Lancaster to those who agreed to build cabins on them and work at their respective trades. It is said that the work of organization went so rapidly that by the spring of 1802, pioneers had settled the land so that the streets and alleys in the central part of Lancaster assumed the shape that is still known today.

I then tried to imagine what it was like for the black people who came to Lancaster to start a new life and to look for the same opportunity as the white settlers. Some of the "colored" settlers were escaped slaves who risked everything to seek their freedom from slavery in the southern states. I asked myself, what was it like, how did they get along with the white settlers, what they did to contribute to the prosperity and growth of Lancaster? What has changed for them over the years?

Even at the time that settlers arrived in Lancaster, there had always been a pro-slavery sentiment in some form, but was said to be generally mild. However, as the slavery sentiment grew and spread throughout the country, the pro-slavery sentiment increased in Lancaster. This was evident in an article written by Herbert M. Turner appearing in the *Lancaster Eagle-Gazette*. Turner stated that in 1848, Joshua Giddings, an anti-slavery apostle, was advertised to speak in Lancaster and a date was set. However, the temper of the people was such that the appointment was withdrawn. Southern sympathy and the strength of "Copperheadism" in Lancaster and Fairfield County often made it difficult for the black citizens in Lancaster.

Lancaster and Fairfield County had several stations on the Underground Railroad, as slaves tried to make their way to Canada. Beyond the upper edge of the Mason-Dixon Line, just above

Kentucky, lies Ohio with the border of the Ohio River, the dividing line between freedom and slavery. Many slaves crossed into Cincinnati from Kentucky, where they received assistance from freed colored people and white sympathizers in their escape. Ohio was also filled with whites who sympathized with the Southern cause and hunted for escaped slaves in order to return them to the South for a bounty. It is reported that sometimes they kidnapped freed blacks and sold them back into slavery.

Heavy penalties were imposed on any citizen of Ohio who was found guilty of supplying food, shelter, or otherwise giving aid to a fugitive slave. Southern Ohio was crawling with secret agents who were alert to detect any violation of the law. Lancaster was no different. However, there were a number of Lancaster and Fairfield County residents who risked their lives to help runaway slaves along the Underground Railroad.

The home of Dr. Michael Effinger was a prominent station and was located in the southwest corner of Main and Broad streets. Dr. Effinger's office was also located in his home. It is said that a large washhouse containing a large brick oven was located at the house. The upstairs contained four small rooms where slaves reportedly were often hidden. At other times, slaves reportedly slept on piles of buffalo robes that Dr. Effinger kept in his doctor's office for that purpose. The home is no longer standing.

Dr. Effinger was said to have been good friends with John Brown, the famous abolitionist. Brown was said to have visited with Dr. Effinger on two occasions in 1859 in the interest of the Underground Railroad. At the time of his visits, Brown sported a Moses-like beard to help disguise his identity because of the large price on his head for his capture. On one visit, he slept in one of the small rooms in the washhouse. The other time he slept in the main house, but his preference was to be with the slaves. In his book *Fairfield County Remembered*, Herbert Turner wrote that Brown left a rare portrait of himself with Dr. Effinger and inscribed on the back, "Your friend, John Brown."

Dr. Effinger was the son of Samuel Effinger who befriended and employed Scipio Smith, a former slave. More of these two will be mentioned later in the book.

Other locations in Lancaster were also reported to be stations on the Underground Railroad. One is The Georgian, also known as The McCracken House, located at the corner of Broad and Mulberry streets. Another station was the Allen Chapel A.M.E. Church when it faced High Street at the corner of Walnut Street. I recall some years ago that a house located at the corner of Chestnut and High streets was being renovated. The owners found several hidden rooms and noted that is was part of the Underground Railroad. Several other locations along Main, Broad and High streets were reported to be a part of the Underground Station, some of which have either been torn down or closed over. I was told that the Fairfield Federal Savings and Loan parking lot on Broad Street was a site that was closed over.

Rushville, another prominent stopping point on the Underground Railroad, reportedly received passengers who traveled through Lancaster and one or more stations northwest of Logan. Research by Deward Watts, a local history buff and a member of the Fairfield Heritage Association, listed the routes of the Underground Railroad through Fairfield County. The routes reportedly roughly followed U.S. Route 22 from the west through Lancaster and on to Rushville; State Route 37 from Lancaster to Granville; old US Route 33 from Logan to Lancaster; and State Route 664 from Logan to Bremen, Rushville, Thornville, and on to Newark.

Watts also stated a route ran from the farm owned by Jonathan Dresbach, located about six miles southeast of Circleville to another rural station kept by a Quaker whose last name was Griffith. The station was located in southwest Fairfield County, about 10 miles northeast of Dresbach's farm. The route, according to Watts, continued 10 miles more to Lancaster and then another 11 miles to Rushville. There, this route was joined by a line north from an active station a little northwest of Logan, which was about 18 miles south of Rushville. About five miles from Rushville is Bremen, which was another busy center for passengers. The passengers coming through Rushville could continue north through the Winegardner region and Thornville, past the east end of the reservoir in Licking County to the Fairmount farm, which was on the route east to Putnam, which is now South Zanesville, with a shortcut northwest to Granville.

The homes of Rev. William Hanby and Dr. Simon Hyde, both of Rushville were used to house fugitive slaves. Dr. Hyde reportedly gave medical treatment to sick and wounded escaped slaves in his office which was on the second floor of his home.

The late Chuck Fisher, a columnist with the *Lancaster Eagle-Gazette*, wrote an article about Rev. Hanby and Dr. Hyde after talking with Hyde's great-great-grandson, Lawrence Hyde. This article appeared in the *Lancaster Eagle-Gazette* on Feb. 18, 1984.

In the article, Fisher wrote that Simon Hyde migrated from Connecticut to Rushville about 1810. He built a brick house on Main Street in Rushville in 1830 and a small office on the east side of the house. Rev. Hanby had a house south of Rushville and operated a harness shop. Hyde and Hanby became the two key figures in the Rushville Underground Railroad. There were reportedly at least seven homes in the area that were runaway slave depots. Fisher wrote that during the operational years of the Underground Railroad, at least seven escaped slaves died and were buried at the Pleasant Hill Cemetery. One of these slaves from Kentucky was Joe Selby, a mulatto who contracted pneumonia and was being treated by Dr. Hyde. Eventually Joe became a most well-known slave because, before he died, according to Fisher, he told Hyde, Hanby, and Hanby's son Benjamin, who was just home from college in Westerville about his sweetheart. Nellie Grey. Joe said that Nellie was a beautiful quadroon who was sold down the river from the plantation next to where Joe was a slave. According to the article, Joe wanted to reach Canada so that he could earn enough money to buy her freedom. However, he only lived a few days and was buried in the Rushville cemetery. He was 22 years old.

Joe's story inspired Benjamin Hanby, who was then a young teacher in Rushville, to compose the words and music to the ballad "Darling Nellie Gray." He was said to have been very much taken with the black girl who was carried away to slavery and thought it was a sad and beautiful story that had to be recorded. While writing the song, Benjamin reportedly would frequently tell his students about the verse he was working on at the time.

When it was finished, the song was first sung in the Rushville school. The song soon swept the nation, and was used to help arouse the North against the institution of slavery.

Fisher wrote that Dr. Hyde was often visited by slave bounty hunters. He kept a human skeleton suspended in a wardrobe at the head of the stairs. He was said to have instructed his children to leave the closet door open, so that strangers who came to the house would see it if they climbed the stairs. He quoted Lawrence Hyde as saying that the skeleton in the closet always worked on slave hunters because of their belief that blacks would never be near such a thing.

I have been told that, during the Civil War years, there was much contention in the community about the war and its issues, which was fueled by the strong rivalry between the staunchly Republican newspaper *Gazette*, and the *Eagle*, long affiliated with the Democrats.

Herbert Turner wrote that while the *Gazette* missed no opportunities to boast of the Union Army's victories, it mustered little enthusiasm for President Lincoln's Emancipation Proclamation. The *Gazette* printed an editorial which supported the emancipation only as a means of defeating the South and not as an act of simple justice or morality towards the slaves. The *Gazette* also wrote that the slaves, freed or not, would never be equal with whites.

The *Eagle*, on the other hand, reportedly blamed all the violence and death entirely on the Republican Party and denounced President Lincoln as a tyrant and dictator.

Later, the *Eagle* reportedly denounced the Emancipation Proclamation and had bitter words to say bout the Union's decision to recruit black soldiers. According to Turner (1999), an editorial was said to have stated that the "Negro was a barbarian and that the Negro's method of war as to massacre women and children, along with men" (p. 65).

Of course, these were false accusations. Many of the white soldiers reportedly wanted nothing to do with the black soldiers during the early years of the Civil War. As the war progressed, black troops proved themselves to be equal in battle and, at times, encountered and overcame heavy Confederate odds. But, it was an uphill battle for the black soldiers to get to that point.

The first black regiment recruited in Ohio was the 127th Ohio Volunteer Infantry at Camp Delaware. Beginning in 1863, the first companies reportedly were trained and continued providing units for the newly named 5th Regiment U.S, Colonel Infantry (USCI) until January 1864. Despite their training, they most often ended up as labor and service troops. The black troops were also paid a smaller wage than the white troops. The blacks received $10 a month compared to $13 a month to the whites. This was not rectified until 1864.

Dwight Barnes wrote about black Civil War soldiers from Lancaster in an article which appeared in the *Lancaster Eagle-Gazette* on February 28, 1996, stating that it was difficult to tell how many black Civil War soldiers are buried in the local cemeteries because of the burial records of veterans are inconclusive. Although most black soldiers are buried in Elmwood Cemetery, located at 300 Mt. Pleasant

Avenue, a number lay beside their white Union brothers-in-arms.

On the cemetery's southern border next to Lawrence Street are graves of seven Civil War black soldiers. Dwight described the following men by using available information from their headstones and military and burial records:

Cpl Joseph Blanchard - Company H, 5th USCI; entered service June 23, 1861, and mustered out with company September 20, 1865. He was listed as a "substitute" (a man paid to replace another for military service) in the National Archive records in Washington, D.C. His wife, Catherine, is buried next to him.

> Pvt. William A. Strawder - Company H, 5th USCI
>
> Pvt. Lemuel Grason - Company H, 5th USCI
>
> Pvt. Henry Green - 1847-1886, Company C, 5th USCI. He is buried next to his mother.
>
> Pvt. Daniel Lest - 1841-1904, Company C, 5th USCI; entered service June 22, 1863, and mustered out with company September 20, 1865. He is buried next to his wife, Malissa.
>
> Sgt. William H. Mallory - Company H, 5th USCI
>
> James Webster - Feb. 28, 1829 to Jan. 21, 1902, 5th USCI.
>
> Pvt. James Walker - 1821 to Dec. 12, 1897, Company E, 27th USCI.

Walker's grave site has a larger headstone than most of the identified USCI soldiers buried in Elmwood Cemetery.

According to Dwight, an obituary was written on Walker appeared in the *Lancaster Eagle* on Dec. 13, 1897. It read "Born a slave in Orange County, Virginia, he arrived in Lancaster in 1869 and was known locally as 'Uncle Jimmie.' In 1895, he was admitted to the Soldiers' Home in Dayton, for an illness not identified in the article, until March 1897, when he returned to Lancaster. He was believed to be recovering here over the next months until his death at age 77 on a Sunday at 1:45 p.m.

Now that I have examined some of the lesser known details regarding the black community of the town, allow me to go back to the early years of the settling of Lancaster and Fairfield County. Herbert M. Turner, in his book *Fairfield County Remembered*, related an incident about a 17-year-old black man who traveled west with the explorer Christopher Grist. The traveling party arrived in Hockhocking, a small town on the site of what is now Lancaster on January 19, 1751 and stayed one night there. The town consisted of four or five Delaware Indian families. The youth was the first recorded black to visit this area.

The Rev. David Jones, a Baptist minister, was recorded to have visited the area in 1773. He reportedly visited a small town comprised of Shawnee and Delaware Indians, whose chief was a Shawnee woman. According to Turner, this chief had several blacks who were taken from Virginia in an earlier war, and were considered to be her property. There were a small number of other blacks among the Indians, possibly all of whom were prisoners.

From what I have been told by the older black adults, the first black pioneers came to this area with their former masters from Virginia and other southern states as early as 1810. There also were a number of slaves who were granted their freedom and decided to come to Lancaster. However, it was not easy for them to do so. Watts reported that Ohio had a Black Code which imposed heavy restrictions on freed slaves. Watts said the Black Codes of 1804 and 1807 stated that blacks and mulattos had to be registered, have $500 bond, and the signature of two white men in order to settle in Ohio.

Watts' research revealed a listing of early black settlers to the Lancaster area. He reported the first black to settle in the area was a black girl, a slave, who was brought to Fairfield County in 1799 by General James Wells, along with his family. Wells settled near the town of Hooker in Greenfield Township. According to an article written by Herbert M. Turner which appeared in the *Lancaster Eagle-Gazette*, Wells never freed the girl. Turner wrote that Wells' will, dated 1814, had the following provision: "I so also give and bequeath unto my two sons and two daughters as above mentioned, a Negro girl, which is to be sold and equally divided."

Other early black residents included a 14-year-old slave girl purchased by Jacob Claypool in Virginia for $250. In his book, Turner wrote that the girl was brought into Fairfield County when Jacob bought the Yankeetown settlement from three squatters. She was granted her freedom.

Sometime in the 1840s, an 18-year-old slave girl was purchased by Jacob's son, Isaac Claypool, in Virginia for $300. Isaac brought her back to Yankeetown, where she met and married Henry Black. They lived in one of the cabins in Yankeetown.

James Boy recorded himself on the Court of Common Pleas in June of 1804, and Isaac Wood recorded himself in May of 1805. Other early black residents include William Peters and Elijah Lewis from Virginia, who settled in Lancaster in 1823. Arriving in Lancaster with Elijah was his father, Daniel Lewis, brother, Stephan Lewis and his wife, known as Aunt Judy (Jones) Lewis, and his sister, known as Aunt Disa Lewis. Aunt Disa boasted of having nursed George Washington when he was a baby. Ruben Banks came in 1814; Others listed included Nelson Smith, a barber; Father Jenkins and Aunty Jenkins; Black Ike and Basil Green, who both lived with the Philemon Beecher family; Yellow Jim, who lived with Parson Wright; Charley Graves; Frank Anderson; Bill Davis; Richard Marcus; Father Watson; John Mathews; Mack Turner, a blacksmith; and John Ampy Jones, a well digger. John reportedly lost his life by "the damps," breathing in toxic gas from a well on the Dunbar farm,

Not all the black settlers were former slaves, however. I have been told that a significant number of blacks emigrated from the New England states, Pennsylvania, and West Virginia. They were intelligent, productive and popular citizens who made contributions to the settlement of this town. It is my understanding that several well-known black families who currently live in Lancaster can trace their roots back to these early pioneers and others who came to this area in the mid- to latter part of the 1800s.

One such lineage is traced back to George Washington DeLoche, who was said to have run away from the DeLoche Plantation located in the Tennessee Valley around 1863. He was supposedly about 12 years old when he met up with

General William Tecumseh Sherman, a Lancaster native, and his Union troops. Sherman befriended George and allowed him to follow his troops as a boot boy. At the end of the Civil War in 1865, Sherman returned to Lancaster with George, who was then about 14 years old. Sherman took George into his home and provided him with an education. Several years later, Sherman moved his wife and family to New York and left George in the care of his brother, Senator Charles Sherman.

While young George was moving around the South with Sherman's troops, his parents and siblings had been emancipated. Mary Margaret DeLoche Hooper and her husband, Joseph "Papa" Hooper were eager to find their son, praying that he was still alive and was able to flee to safety and freedom. The Hoopers traveled around looking for him. Somehow, they were able to trace George to Lancaster.

Charles Sherman did not want full responsibility of caring for George. When the Hoopers found Charles, he returned George to his family but acted as the family's guardian. Charles helped the Hoopers to settle in Lancaster. They indentured themselves in order to gain property on what is now Forest Rose Avenue. Papa Hooper worked as a blacksmith on this property.

George became an apprentice to a barber. At the age of 17, George met and married a 15-year-old girl by the name of Mary Margaret. George was a successful barber; however, later in life he and Mary operated a general store. The DeLoches had nine children, including Jen DeLoche, who grew up and eventually married William H. Thomas. "Aunt" Jen was a hairdresser.

Jen and William had four daughters from their marriage, all who were well-known in Lancaster: Ruth Thomas Jeffries, Lucille Thomas Brown, Florence Thomas Trotter and Mary Thomas Ulmer Campbell. I have been told that Mary's first husband produced her only child, Jennmary Ulmer Boyd, who currently lives in Columbus where she was a practicing podiatrist. She graduated from the Ohio College of Podiatry in Cleveland with a degree of Doctor of Podiatry in May 1945.

Mary's second husband, Josh Campbell, was a very familiar face in Lancaster. Josh went into business for himself, shining shoes in 1933. Before that, he worked at the old Mithof Hotel, later known as Milner Hotel. Josh had his own shoeshine shop on North Columbus Street, just a few steps north of Main Street.

When Josh died in 1963, he was deeply mourned by both blacks and whites in Lancaster. An article was written about his death in the *Lancaster Eagle-Gazette*.

In addition to George DeLoche, there were two other black barbers in Lancaster at that time: Robert Randall and John Gardner. I was told that Robert came to Lancaster with General Sherman and his troops after Sherman's famous "March to the Sea" during the Civil War. He operated his barbershop at 237 West Main Street for many years.

According to an article in the *Lancaster Eagle-Gazette* dated Oct. 25, 1962 called "Lancaster Happenings" which were news bits taken from the *Daily Eagle* files, Robert Randall told a reporter that he was born on a plantation near Guthrie, Georgia. His father was free man, and his mother was a slave. Robert reported that he witnessed his mother being whipped by a slave driver when she paused in a field to rest. He also recalled that Col. Joseph Murray, owner of the plantation fell over dead when he received word that Atlanta had fallen.

According to the article, Robert, who was 13 years old at the time, served as an orderly for Dr. Peter Hewetson of Amanda, Ohio when the Union troops stopped at the Murray plantation. He later worked for Capt. Henry Beck, also of Amanda, who commanded Company I, 43rd Regiment (many of the soldiers were from Fairfield County). The company brought Robert to Lancaster with them. Robert told the reporter that he remembered Gen. Sherman as a kindly man who was strictly military.

John Gardner was said to have come from Arkansas sometime in the 1860s. He established his barbershop on North Broad Street where the Shaw's Inn is now located.

Chapter 2

Churches as the Center of the Black Community

The early black setters had the opportunity to own land just as the white settlers. However, they were only encouraged to buy land and live on the south end of the city. This land was on the edge of what was wilderness in the early 1800s.

Segregation was a fact of life in Lancaster, not as much as by law as it was in the South, but more by custom. Where the blacks could buy land and live was proof of this fact. I do not know exactly how much land these settlers owned. I have been told that the black citizens did own the land from High Street at Walnut Street south to the railroad tracks: all of Locust Street to Maple Street Maple Street to the 700 block of Maple Street all of the land along the Hocking River and down and around Elmwood Park and Cemetery. This is the area where my family made their homes and where I grew up. A number of the same families still live in this area.

In addition to being segregated as to where they lived, the black settlers were not permitted to attend worship services at white churches, nor could the children attend the same school as the white students. Let is find out first about the educational situation in Lancaster.

It is my understanding that separate schools for the black students below the high school level were maintained until the end of the1885-86 school year. Colored students at that time were permitted to attend the white high school in 1878. Up to that time, students went to a brick schoolhouse that was built on the western part of the North Elementary School grounds. After the black and white schools combined, the building was used as a janitor's residence and later became the Athletic Field House until it was torn down.

In addition to North School, the people of the South District voted in 1850 to share an improved school system with the North District. The first South School was completed and opened to students on April 1, 1851. The location of the school was on four acres of land situated outside the city limits. It had eight rooms and two stories. In 1856, the high school moved into South School because of the overcrowded conditions at North School. Classes were continued until 1873.

It was reported that in 1857, school was suspended in the colored grade school because of the lack of a sufficient number of students. School was made available again in 1859 for a five-month term per year.

In 1869, the congregation of the black church, which we will talk about later in this chapter, sold a piece of land on

Walnut Street to the City of Lancaster to build a new South School facility. One stipulation made by the church was that the black children must be allowed to attend classes at the new school. Additional land was purchased from Patrick and Mary Powers. The second South Elementary School, which contained twelve rooms and three floors, was completed in 1875. It was opened to both black and white students in September of that year.

The construction of the third South School building was started on April 14, 1930 and was opened to students on January 5, 1931. It was dedicated on February 20, 1931. The school remains much the same today, with the exception of a new kitchen which was built in the mid-1960s.

In addition to adequate school facilities for the black children, several of the early leading black citizens felt it was only fair that the black citizens should have an established place to worship. Among them was Scipio Smith.

Deward Watts was able to find out information about Scipio Smith in order to do a character sketch for a Black History Walk. This special event sponsored by the Fairfield Heritage Association and the Black Interest Group of Lancaster was held in April 2005.

Scipio Smith was once a slave of Benjamin Smith of Rockingham, Virginia. Benjamin decided to move to Ohio. Before leaving Virginia, he freed all of his slaves. Scipio came to Ohio in 1810 under the sponsorship of Benjamin Smith and Samuel Effinger. Scipio and Samuel became very close friends and had much respect for each other. In 1812, Samuel employed Scipio as a journeyman tinsmith and coppersmith, which made Scipio the first black man to enter business in Lancaster. In 1827, after Samuel's death, Scipio reportedly started his own business.

According to research, Scipio, who was said to have been very dark-skinned, very muscular man, was quite tall – 6'4". In the book *Fairfield County Remembered* by Herbert Turner, Scipio was said to have been as "stout as a horse and could hold his side of a double tree, even with the best animal that ever pulled against him."

It was reported that Scipio lost one of his legs as a youth and sported a wooden leg. He was self-taught and became well educated. He was known throughout the community for his kindness, especially towards children.

Scipio married Sarah Johnson, who was from Washington D.C., on May 2, 1833. They had one daughter, Elizabeth, who grew up and married a schoolteacher by the name of Dan Brown.

Scipio and his family lived in their home located on the west side of Perry Street and south of Walnut Street. The Smiths eventually took in boarders while they worked to make enough money to buy their own lot on Walnut or Locust streets or one of the other streets on the south end of town. The 1850 census listed these boarders as Woodruff, age 25, a blacksmith; Samuel Johnson, 19, a blacksmith; David Brown, 28, a grocer; Rachel Brown, 26; and Theodore Walker, 29. Scipio eventually renamed himself Scipio Africanus. He died sometime between 1855 and 1859.

A deeply spiritual man, Scipio was concerned with the religious needs of the black citizens. He was aware of and interested in the founding of the African Methodist Episcopal

(A.M.E.) denomination. He read about how colored people were thrown out of a Methodist Church in Philadelphia. Rev. Richard Allen and Absalom Jones were the leaders of those people, who formed the A.M.E. Church. Smith approached Emmanuel Carpenter, a leading white citizen who owned much land in Lancaster, about donating land to the black community in order to build a church and school.

Allow me to pause and explain who Emmanuel Carpenter was and his role in helping the black community. Emmanuel Carpenter arrived in the Lancaster area in 1799 with his father, who bought some of the lots from Zane. The Carpenter family was active in the local business community and owned several mills and other businesses in the area. Emmanuel was a survey who became the county Sheriff in the early 1800s. He eventually purchased the remaining 437 acres of Zane's lots and called it Carpenter's Addition, with the plan to make it the center of Lancaster. He dedicated three parcels for church and graveyard purposes.

In 1814, at the insistence of his uncle, Samuel Carpenter, who was an Old School Baptist preacher, Emmanuel gave the black people of the Baptist denomination a strip of land between Pearl Avenue and High Street. They built a log cabin which stood in the center of what is now Walnut Street.

Emmanuel sold the other half of the lot for $1 to the Methodist Episcopal Church. The congregation built a church and used part of the land as a cemetery. This is now the location of the Masonic Temple.

After talking extensively with Scipio Smith, Emmanuel and Scipio made an agreement. Scipio was to wait to see if the Baptist Church would be successful. If so, he would join them. If they failed, Scipio would be free to start whatever church he wanted. Once the church proved that the membership would be permanent, and they obtained the funds to build a permanent structure, the land would be deeded to them. Emmanuel said he would stipulate that a school would also be erected and that no land speculator would ever take the land from the colored citizens of Lancaster.

The Baptist congregation was unable to sustain their church, and it was abandoned. The year is unknown to me. In 1825, Scipio and other colored citizens took over the land and formed the A.M.E. Church. Scipio was the church's first minister. I was told that Scipio's powerful, resonant voice was heard from the A.M.E. meeting house to the remotest edges of town. It was said that when he sang, he kept the beat of the song with his wooden leg. I remember hearing stories about Indians who lived deeper in the wilderness would come to the edge of the wilderness to listen to the singing and preaching during the services.

Under the leadership of Scipio, the church prospered and became part of the Chillicothe Circuit, which included Chillicothe, Zanesville, Cincinnati, and Lancaster. I also was told by several people that the A.M.E. church was a station for the Underground Railroad. Runaway slaves from Kentucky and Virginia sought safety at the church as they made their way to Canada.

In 1869, the congregation received help from the City of Lancaster and other interested citizens, and a permanent two-story building was erected. It was at the corner of High and Walnut streets, and faced High Street. The ground floor was used for school, and the second floor was used for church services. Mr. Guy was the first teacher of the school. Also, on the ground floor under the two stairwells were two rooms: one room was as a sleeping and living quarters for the minister and his family, and the other room was used as a kitchen and dining room.

Despite the success of the Allen Chapel A.M.E. congregation and the regularly held services on the land given to them, a quit-claim deed was not granted to the congregation by the city until November 19, 1889. John Viney, George Moss, and Luisa Strander were the church officers. The deed stated that the land cannot be sold by the black citizens of Lancaster and must be used for church and/or school purposes. If the land is declared abandoned and no longer used by the black people of Lancaster, it would revert back to the heirs of Emmanuel Carpenter. The church flourished and remains active today.

John Viney, who was said to be an "upright, honorable and Christian gentleman," was a very active member of the Allen Chapel A.M.E. Church after his arrival in Lancaster in April of 1855. John's date of birth is listed as March 17, 1832 in Pocahontas County, Virginia. His first wife reportedly died in 1857. He later married Chaney Ann Swift on August 29, 1861 in Shelby County, Ohio. John and Chaney had seven children, J. Edmund, Frank, John, William and Emanuel. Edmund later became a trustee of the church and was the superintendent of the Sunday School for several years.

William had the distinction of being the first black person to graduate from Lancaster High School. He was the class valedictorian. It is said that his speech to his classmates and the audience was remembered for many years. William went on to become a principal of the Southern School District of Chillicothe. Emanuel became a Professor of Music in Huntington, West Virginia.

John Viney, who had his own business, white-washing, plastering, house-cleaning, was a general utility man. On March 3, 1863, Viney was granted a license to preach the Gospel at the A.M.E. Church. He is also listed as being a trustee of the church in 1900 along with the minister of the church, said to be Rev. P. Tolliver, who began his pastorate in 1899. The names of members of the Viney family, along with other names including Scott and Anna James are inscribed on the stained glass windows of the church sanctuary.

While Viney was pastor of Allen Chapel A.M.E. Church, the colored citizens, on June 16, 1870, held a celebration of the 15th Amendment, which gave the blacks the right to vote and to hold public office. Large delegations came from areas including Columbus, Zanesville, Circleville, and Washington, Court House. The celebration was also held to raise money for the building of a permanent church structure. This celebration was much more peaceful and successful than the Emancipation Day celebration in 1848.

Many people came from out of town to join the Lancaster black community in celebration of the anniversary of the West Indian Emancipation, which was disguised as a Sunday School celebration. Great preparations were made for the event, which was held on the first day of August, John B. Reed painted banners, and the church congregation worked so that all things were ready for the displays. However, the festivities came to a quick end when a group of the town's "rowdies" chased the delegation out of Lancaster. It is said that, at midnight of July 31, the eve of the celebration, the home of Nelson Smith, which was considered to be the headquarters of the black people, was mobbed by the rough elements of Lancaster. Nelson's home was badly wrecked and the furniture was destroyed. The 100 or more black visitors from Chillicothe and Circleville quickly left town. Dan Brown, Scipio Smith's son-in-law and a school teacher, drew his rifle on one of the leaders of the mob. However, Mrs. Nelson Smith prevented him from shooting the man.

William Slade, son of the ex-governor of Vermont, and cashier of the Hocking Valley Bank, was the only man in town who was brave enough to denounce the violence on the black community, which he reportedly did in very vigorous language. Henry Stanbery, former Lancaster resident and attorney general of Ohio was in town on a visit. Stanbery reproved Slade for his actions. It was necessary for a guard to be placed around Slade's house that night to prevent any retaliation by white residents for Slade's actions.

Another peaceful and, this time, a successful event for the black community was held in January of 1876. A number of black residents gathered at City Hall to participate in a "cake walk." Contestants, dressed in their very best clothing, fancifully walked to the music provided by a local band, the Andy Lilly String Band, past judges to win the prize of a cake. Richard Marcus, a former slave from Virginia who purchased his freedom, was the winner of the cake.

Viney was very much respected in the Lancaster community. He was selected to serve as a member of the jury on three different occasions, something that was almost unheard of at that time. Viney reportedly got to know John Brassee, one of Lancaster's prominent attorneys, while doing some work for him. Brassee reportedly asked Viney to serve on a jury to decide the fate of a man arrested for murder. After that, he was asked to serve on a jury to hear a murder trial. Viney was said to have remained active in the church and the community until his death sometime after 1910.

In addition to Scipio Smith and John Viney, other early ministers of Allen Chapel A.M.E. include Rev. Grey, Rev. Thomas Lawrence, Rev. Samuel J. Clingman, Rev. Lafayette Davis, Rev. C.H. Peters, Rev. George Coleman, Rev. Thomas Lawrence, Rev. Daniel Winlon; Rev. John P, Woodson; Rev. Jeremiah Bowman; Rev. John Tibbs; Rev. Edward Esse; Rev. John W. Jones; Rev. Arthur Howell; Rev. Isaac Dillon; Rev. Roberts; Rev. Daniel Cooper; Rev. R. Hogan; Rev. William Arnold; Rev. Gibbons; Rev. Lewis; Rev. W. D. Mitchell; Rev. Davidson; Rev. Clark; Rev. R. Morris; Rev. R.M. Wilson; Rev. P. Tolliver; and Rev. J.B. Harewood.

A parsonage was built on the church property at the corner of Pearl Alley and Walnut Street in 1903 under the leadership of Mrs. M.R. Smith, president of the Ladies Auxiliary. Over the years, the parsonage was home to many A.M.E. ministers and their families. It was also occupied at times by families who attended Allen Chapel, including my parents until I was almost two years old. Ruby Fisher and her family also lived in the parsonage. The parsonage was used until the mid-1970s. No longer occupied and in need of repair, the church trustees at that time allowed it to be used as fire training by the Lancaster Fire Department.

The church building underwent a major project in 1914 when the building was turned around to face Walnut Street and was remodeled. The first floor, which was used as a school until South School was completed in 1880 was turned into the Sunday School room, in which case, the blackboards were removed. The area also served as a dining and social room. The rooms once used as the living quarters were made into kitchens. In these kitchens, church members prepared the famous chicken dinners that older citizens of Lancaster still remember. In addition to the dinners, the grounds of Allen Chapel were alive and festive when the congregation held their annual bazaars and barbecues. These events were not limited to the church members, but were attended and enjoyed by the Lancaster community as a whole.

A roster of the local black residents, most of whom were members of the Allen Chapel A.M.E. Church sometime in the 1930s was discovered. It reads as follows, separating the men and women:

> Miss Jennie Thomas, 723 Forest Rose Avenue
>
> Mrs. Catherine Brizzell, 625 E.6th Avenue
>
> Mrs. Julia Allen, Wheeling Hill;
>
> Mrs. Henry Oliver, 1211 E. Walnut Street
>
> Mrs. Hazel Byrd, 145 E. Main Street
>
> Mrs. Floyd Randall, E. Walnut Street
>
> Mrs. Rebecca Randall, 538 E. Locust Street
>
> Mrs. Harriet Nelson, 528 E. Locust Street

Mrs. Stella Childs, 528 E. Locust Street

Mrs. Effie Howell, S. High Street

Mrs. Lyrenna Dills, 436 E. Locust Street

Mrs. Florence Hunster, Lawrence Street

Mrs. Anna Hunster, 612 N. Maple Street

Mrs. Nora Hunster, 612 N. Maple Street

Mrs. Anna Harden, S. Columbus Street

Mrs. Laura Tibbs, 531 E. Chestnut Street

Mrs. Emma Tibbs, 531 E. Chestnut Street

Mrs. Lucy Gardner, Sycamore Street

Miss Francis Harris, 432 E. Wheeling Street

Mrs. Joanna Holmes, 435 E. Wheeling Street

Mrs. Ida Viney, 411 E. Wheeling Street

Mrs. Carrie Wolfe, 403 E. Wheeling Street

Mrs. Lulu Hawkins, Corner of Wheat Street and
the railroad tracks;

Mrs. Jennie Hawkins, 338 E. Locust Street

Mrs. Birdie Carlisle, 334 E. Locust Street

Mrs. Edith Carlisle, 334 E. Locust Street

Mrs. Emma Hawkins, 320 E. Locust Street

Mrs. Anna James, 529 E. Walnut Street

Mrs. Susie Westbrook, 570 E. Locust Street

Mrs. Lizzie Turner, Cedar Hill Road;

Mrs. Bessie Richard, 528 E. Locust Street

Mrs. Anna Tibbs, 1241 S. Broad Street

Mrs. Florence Tibbs, RFD 9 S. Broad Street

Mrs. Ellen Jenkins, the paper mill district;

Mrs. Anderson, 424 E. Mulberry Street

Mrs. Nell Anderson, 420 E. Mulberry Street

Mrs. Daniel Lett, 416 E. Mulberry Street

Mrs. Ada Moss, 408 E. Mulberry Street

Mrs. Bertha Moss, 408 E. Mulberry Street

Mrs. Ethel Moss, 416 E. Mulberry Street

Mrs. Anna Mallory, 404 E. Mulberry Street

Mrs. Dora Cox, 400 E. Mulberry Street

Mrs. Lola Cockran, 400 E. Mulberry Street

Mrs. Edna Carter, 413 E. Mulberry Street

Susie Carter, 413 E. Mulberry Street

Jessie Ball, 413 E. Mulberry Street

Mrs. Jennie Smith, S. Columbus Street

Mrs. Street, 406 E. Locust Street

Mrs. Goldie Clair, Perry Street

Mrs. Mary Carter, S. Columbus Street

Mrs. Phelia Philips, S. Columbus Street

Mrs. Faney Clair, 440 E. Wheeling Street

Mrs. Edna Clair, 361 E. Wheeling Street

Mrs. Clara McLinn, the A.M.E. parsonage

Mrs. Mallie Ford, 406 E. Mulberry Street

Mrs. J. Blanchard, 406 E. Mulberry Street

Mrs. Alice Banks, 430 E. Wheeling Street

Mrs. Bessie Allen, 417 E. Mulberry Street

Mrs. E. Hammond, S. Columbus Street

Mrs. Jane Lewis, 410 E. Mulberry Street

Mrs. G.G. Smith, 416 E. Mulberry Street

Ray Smith, 409 S. Broad Street

Mode Smith, 409 S. Broad Street

Charley Grey, 409 S. Broad Street

Enos J. Streets, 406 E. Locust Street

William Clair, Perry Street

Joshia Canrel, Mithoff Hotel;

Ike Freeman; George Bibbs, 529 E. Walnut Street

Edward Clair, Jr., 361 E. Wheeling Street

Edward Clair, Sr., 440 E. Wheeling Street

Rev. McLinn, A.M.E. parsonage

George Ford, 406 E. Mulberry Street

Henry Hawkins, 338 E. Locust Street

Edward Banks, 430 E. Wheeling Street

Howard Ball, 413 E. Mulberry Street

William Webester, George Webester, Harry Webester, and James Webester, RFD 12;

Herbert Jackson, 400 E. Mulberry Street

William Jackson, 400 E. Mulberry Street

Ralph Streets, 406 E. Locust Street

William Long, Cedar Hill Rd. c/o Mace Turner;

C. W. Cook, Cedar Hill Rd c/o Mace Turner;

Will Thomas, 723 Forest Avenue

John Scott, 625 E. 6th Avenue

Henry Oliver, 1211 E. Walnut Street

Okey Byrd, 145 E. Main Street

Robert Byrd; Robert Randall, 538 E. Locust Street

Walter Randall, 538 E. Locust Street

James Howell, S. High Street

Willie Howell, S. High Street

Jordan Dills, 436 E. Locust Street

Charley Hunster, Lawrence Street

Earl Hunster, 612 N. Maple Street

Fred Tibbs, 531 E. Chestnut Street

Roy Tibbs, 531 E, Chestnut Street

John Gardner, Sycamore Street

John Harris, 432 E. Wheeling Street

Shirley Harris, 432 E. Wheeling Street

Daniel Holmes, 435 E. Wheeling Street

J. Edmond Viney, 411 E. Wheeling Street

Clark Wolfe, 403 E. Wheeling Street

Alcupe Lewis, 405 E. Wheeling Street

Oscar Hawkins, Wheat Street

Frank Hawkins, 338 Locust Street

Noah Carlisle, 334 E. Locust Street

Will Hooper, 320 E. Locust Street

Mr. Sorrell, 334 E. Locust Street

George Hawkins, 320 E. Locust Street

John W. Westbrook, 570 E. Locust Street

Nace Turner, Cedar Hill Road;

Albert Richard, 568 E. Locust Street

Sheridan Tibbs, 1241 S. Broad Street

Albert Tibbs, RFD 9 S. Broad Street

Earl Jenkins, the paper mill district;

John Fisher, S. Columbus Street

George Anderson, 424 E. Mulberry Street

Pearl Anderson, 420 E. Mulberry Street

Harry Strauder, 410 E. Mulberry Street

John Moss, 416 E. Mulberry Street

Harry Moss, 408 E. Mulberry Street

Rube Moss, 408 E. Mulberry Street

John Liggins, 404 E. Mulberry Street

R.W. Anderson, 400 E. Mulberry Street

James Cochran, 400 E. Mulberry Street

Robert Carter, 413 E. Mulberry Street

Harry Carter, 413 E. Mulberry Street

Russell Smith, S. Columbus Street

Egbert Smith, S. Columbus Street

Will Allen, 417 E. Mulberry Street

Edward Webster, 135 E. Chestnut Street

Mr. Hammond, S. Columbus Street.

I do not remember the special church-sponsored events since I was not yet born or was too young to remember. I do recall the big breakfasts served on Easter Sunday after the Sunrise Service. During the service, I always thought God gave us a special day when I saw the sunlight make the stained glass windows sparkle and glow. My dad talked about how, after the Sunrise Service, members of the congregation went to the dining room to enjoy the breakfast cooked by the men of the church. The menu usually consisted of cereal, scrambled eggs, pancakes, sausage, and beverages. Afterwards, the Sunday School classes met, followed by a special Easter church service. After church was over, everyone received candy, and an Easter egg hunt was held for the children. I remember trying to hold onto my hat as I tried to find eggs before the older kids found all of them. It did not matter to me if I got my white gloves dirty or not. I remember that Danny Smith stopped hunting long enough to help me find a few eggs and even put one of his eggs in my basket.

Dolores Carlisle and other adults put together programs for the children to present to the church for these holidays. At Christmas, after the program, my dad passed out candy and treat bags that he had put together for every member of the church. I remember my brothers and I wanted to help Dad, but he refused because he knew we just wanted to sample the candy.

The church was at its height until attendance began to dwindle in the early 1960's. I was told that members were disenchanted when the A.M.E. conference sent some of the ministers who seemed to be more interested in collecting money for the home church than in ministering the Word of God and by members who used the church more as a social hour than to worship God. This was also a time when Martin Luther King, Jr. and many other civil rights freedom fighters in the South forced the federal governments to open the doors of opportunity to blacks that have always been wide open for white citizens. This allowed the black residents of Lancaster to broaden their horizons as the walls of discrimination began to crumble. As a result, the black citizens attended church less frequently and did not need its umbrella to satisfy their socialization needs. Others, especially the younger adults, moved away from Lancaster, to find better jobs after high school or after they graduated from college.

A significant group of people formally broke away from the church in 1967 when a dispute developed between the Allen Chapel congregation and the A.M.E. conference from Wilberforce, Ohio. This group included my parents, Kenneth and Alice Saunders; Emma and Dolores Carlisle; Minnie Saunders; Gladys and Frank Keels; Wilbur and Joan Carlisle, and all their children. This group formed a second black church, which was started in the home of my parents on Locust Street. According to Mom, she was not satisfied with the Biblical teachings offered at Allen Chapel. She wanted to talk to a Bible-based minister to help her get through some type of personal situation. She said she called several churches in Lancaster with no success. Some suggested that she find a minister at a church in Columbus. When she called the local First Baptist Church, she told the woman who answered the church phone that it was okay if she was prejudiced against blacks, that all she wanted was to talk with someone, and she then hung up the phone in frustration. Mom said a man called her back a few minutes later and said he was concerned for her. He scheduled a time for them to get together to talk. The gentleman came to our home, and eventually came once a week to discuss the Bible. They held an informal Bible study. Several other people began to attend the Bible study at Mom's invitation and soon had a roomful of people. They began to meet regularly on Wednesday evenings.

For unknown reasons to us, the gentleman had to leave town shortly after he started meeting with us. Mom said she did not know if it was because members of his church may not have liked the fact that he was teaching blacks. It seemed to the adults that it was acceptable for him to meet with us as long as he did not bring us to their church building.

In order for us to continue to receive help, the gentleman recommended a Pastor Lamb who also attended First Baptist Church. However, Lamb was unable to help the small band of believers. Instead, he sent a young eager pastor by the name of Ronald England.

Brother England, as we called him, appeared to be a little different from the others who attended the First Baptist Church-- it did not seem to bother him that he was the only white person in the small group who met on Locust Street. Perhaps it was because his wife, Elena, was a native of Hawaii.

Regardless of his reason, Brother England continued to hold Wednesday night Bible study. The group grew in numbers. After a period of time, Brother England encouraged the adults to withdraw from Allen Chapel A.M.E. to form their own church.

It was about 1963 or 1964 when close to 20 people formally left Allen Chapel A.M.E. and formed Grace Baptist Church. Brother England agreed to be the pastor of the church and left First Baptist Church.

Establishing another black church was not without its problems. I remember Brother England took us to First Baptist Church for a Sunday evening service. The service had already started when we arrived. When we walked in the sanctuary and people noticed us, it became very quiet.

I remember the music stopped, the singing stopped, and every head turned towards the back to look at us. I recall wondering why everyone was staring at us and wanted to turn around and run from the church. I did not want to go any further. Mom and Dad told us to keep walking to our seats. When we sat down, the service resumed. However, no one talked to us or greeted us after the service. I was in the fourth or fifth grade at the time. This incident made a negative impression on me for a long time.

The summer following that incident, the congregation's idea of associating with blacks seemed to change a little. The young people of Grace Baptist were invited to attend Vacation Bible School at First Baptist Church. I do not recall specifics about it. I have to admit I was somewhat scared and apprehensive, but I also remember having fun. I remember the first person who ran to our car to greet us was Pastor Lamb's daughter, Becky. She was so nice to us and made me feel comfortable. Becky and I became good friends.

During my sixth year at the elementary school, 1965-66, members of Grace Baptist Church were invited to attend Pine Lake Baptist Camp in Caldwell, Ohio. I had heard stories from my school friends about summer camp and I really wanted to go. Besides, Becky was going and had already asked me to see if I could go as well. Brother England held a contest to see who would receive a scholarship to attend a week-long camp. My cousin, Wendy Keels and I tied, so they paid for both of us to go. We did not experience any problems and made many friends. I was selected as Camper of the Week and received a trophy. I went back to the camp the next year and had just as much fun, especially reuniting with Becky and another friend, Kirby Lancaster. If I remember correctly, Kirby was awarded Camper of the Week that year. I remember there was a terrible hayride accident towards the end of the week. The brakes of the tractor went out as we went down a big hill, and the two wagons jack-knifed. There were a number of teens and several counselors who were injured. I was thrown clear and lost consciousness. Kirby was the first person I saw when I came to again, and he was making sure I was okay. Although he suffered a broken leg himself, he assisted many people before he was taken to the hospital. I injured my leg and shoulder. Becky helped me get around for the remaining time. When we left Pine Lake Camp and arrived back at the First Baptist Church, this was the last time I saw Becky and Kirby. I will never forget their kindness and friendship.

The congregation of Grace Baptist Church moved around to different homes. My parents had the Wednesday night Bible study; Emma and Dolores Carlisle had the Sunday morning services; and my grandmother, Minnie Saunders, had Sunday night services. Eventually, Brother England held Sunday morning services at his house on Rainbow Drive. At that time, this was an area where blacks were not permitted to live. I remember the England's house caught fire and we had to move services to another home. I think it was about 1967. The church rented one side of a duplex on East Mulberry Street. It was not until 2005 that I found out from Steve Conrad, a white friend who is friends with the England family that the fire was not accidental. It was reportedly firebombed by whites who lived in the area as a way to protest having black people in the England's' home.

Brother England and Elena never talked to us about the incident.

After several years of holding services in the Mulberry Street duplex, Grace Baptist Church purchased a building on Winding Street. The membership of Grace Baptist Church maintained an active level although it never grew big in numbers. My parents made the decision to leave Grace Baptist in the early 1970s for personal reasons.

Several years later, Brother England and his family left the church. They eventually became associated with Calvary Baptist Church in Lancaster, where my friend, Kirby Lancaster was pastor at one time. On June 9, 1982, Ron and Elena were commissioned as missionaries to Hawaii. A special Aloha Sunday was held at Calvary Baptist Church. A musical program was held in the morning with a special message delivered by Pastor Lancaster. Following the service, a Hawaiian luau was held. The formal commissioning service was held that evening with the ceremony of the "Laying on of Hands" to send the Englands to build a work in Honokaa where Baptist Mid-missions began a baby church. All members of Grace Baptist Church were invited to attend. The Englands left for Hawaii on June 13, 1983. They continue to live and work for God in Hawaii, and maintain their home in Lancaster, making at least annual visits.

Several ministers led the church over the years including Kenneth Leeper, James Parker, Eugene Turner and Ron Thomas, a white minister.

Overt racism and racial discrimination were no longer prevalent, and more doors of opportunities opened for the black community. More black citizens moved away to live elsewhere or to attend college, while others were welcomed to attend white churches. As a result, the membership of both Allen Chapel A.M.E. and Grace Baptist fell dropped dramatically and never recovered. Grace Baptist Church closed its doors in 2000, and the property was sold to the family of Mike Dexter, who was a black pastor of Good Shepherd Church, a predominately white congregation. It was used for a private Christian School until it was sold in 2005. Further history of Allen Chapel A.M.E., I believe, warrants its own section.

Chapter 3

Allen Chapel A.M.E. Church

We have already established in the previous chapter that segregation was a part of Lancaster's unwritten but understood rule. In most parts of the United States, it was against the law for blacks to participate in activities and to go places that the white people always took for granted. This meant that the black citizens not only lived in the same area and attended the same church, but they also socialized together. Thus, Allen Chapel A.M.E. Church was an integral part of Lancaster's black community, socially as well as spiritually.

For the families, especially during the 1940s until the '60s, the church sponsored ice cream socials with home-made ice cream, cakes and pies. Sunday afternoon Gospel Sings which featured out-of-town choirs were held on a regular basis. Dolores Carlisle talked about the evening lantern socials that were held in the summers. She said church members strung up lamps and lanterns between the church and the parsonage which made a beautiful sight as the sun went down and it grew darker. They offered refreshments and entertainment for those in attendance.

Another popular event was the annual Fall Festival that was held on the church lot. Joan Carlisle told me stories about how her father, Rube Moss, along with Rollie Fisher and other volunteers made long tables from sawhorses and boards for the festival. She said they had games, bingo, and other entertainment to enjoy. Months before the day of the event, the women of the church held quilting bees and auctioned off the quilts that they made at the festival.

Allen Chapel was well-known throughout the city for their chicken dinners held at the church. People placed their orders ahead of time and then either ate at the church or took the dinners home. In the summer, the men of the church barbequed chicken on homemade grills while the women sold pies and cakes during the meal. Many of the older people recall the church's equally delicious chicken pie sales. Once a year, members took orders in the community and delivered the dinners on the designated date. It took members several days to cook the chicken and the make 9-inch pies. Joan said they sold the pies with a 1-quart container of gravy.

The Sunday School picnics were something the younger church members looked forward to in the summers. Joan said her father, Rube, who owned the Lancaster Transference and Storage Company, placed chairs in the big moving van to take church members and their plentiful picnic baskets to Rising Park. After the younger people ate and rested, Rube loaded them up in the van again and took them to swim at Clearcreek.

For the youth, Allen Chapel sponsored Sunday School picnics, Halloween and Christmas parties, talent shows. They also included contests with a chance to pantomime to records or lip-synch.

The adults were not to be left out. Several clubs grew out of the Allen Chapel congregation which answered the black adults' need for acceptance and social fulfillment. The clubs and groups included the Bon Ami, Club, Decum Club, Fortnightly Club, and the Say and Do Club.

A group of 15 to 20 young women between the ages of 20 to 35 years formed the Bon Ami (French for "good friend") Club for purely social reasons. Among their activities was an annual Cabaret talent show. The club lasted between 8 and 10 years.

The Fortnightly Club was in existence from 1940 until 1966. The club started in the home of Jennie Thomas. The other original members included Mrs. Bowser, Mrs. Cooper, Ethel Hawkins, Ada Moss, and Alka Steele.

The activities were considered to be beneficial to the members and to others, and were largely educational or cultural in nature. Some of the activities and projects were said to include visits to soldiers at Lockbourne Air Force Base in Columbus and in Chillicothe. Members volunteered to roll bandages for the local American Red Cross. They also held bake sales to raise money for the YM-YWCA Building Fund.

Interestingly they would raise money for the YM-YWCA despite the fact that they were not permitted to attend the activities. I was told that Mary Burnham, who was associated with the YWCA, was instrumental in providing activities for the black youth of the 1950s and '60s. Whenever the Y facilities were available, she made sure the black teens were allowed to hold dances and parties there. Because she knew Dad was a responsible adult and a Sunday School teacher, Mary often entrusted my dad to chaperone the dances and parties, and to clean up afterwards.

The membership of the Fortnightly Club changed as the years passed. Down through the years of the club, as one member dropped out, she was replaced, thereby keeping their number at ten to twelve members. Mrs. Bowser was said to be the first charter member to leave when she moved away from town. She was replaced by Miss Edith Howell. Mrs. Mary Carlisle resigned on May 14, 1962 and was replaced by Mrs. Olive Smith on June 11, 1962.

Minutes to the club's 20th anniversary celebration, dated Nov. 13, 1960, were found to be of interest:

Tonight we gathered at the home of Miss Rosalie Booker to enjoy a luscious dinner of Cornish hens, prepared by her (the rest of the delicious menu contributed and prepared among the rest of the members).

Upon arrival we found Miss Booker's apartment abounding with gala atmosphere. Bright balloons clinging to walls and ceiling, gay little favors waiting for each member.

The table was a picture in itself, lovely linen, silver and glassware (illegible) by a beautiful; centerpiece of green and white carnations (our club colors) with English ivy surrounded by four tall, slim white tapers, a gift presented by Miss Evelyn Kaumeyer.

Near-by and lavishly arrayed with all things necessary to liquid refreshment was the cocktail table. We each availed ourselves of our favorite stimulant, and held lively conversation until dinner was ready.

Just as we were seated, Mr. Stanley Carlisle took pictures of the group. We partook of the luscious meal, engaged in much happy reminiscing and then toasted our twenty years together.

After the meal, we had the revealing of secret sisters, in the midst of delighted squeals and hearty thank yous for lovely gifts we discovered who had been each one's sister for the year. Then we drew names for next year's sister.

And after that, far into the night we continued to enjoy our celebration.

The 1961-62 roll call for the Fortnightly Club included Bessie Allen, Edith Ball, Rosalie Booker, Malva Brown, Mary Carlisle, Mary Nichols, Verna Preston, Ruth Ely, and Olive Smith. Many of these women stayed with the club until it was disbanded in 1966.

The Decum Club was formed about the same time as the Fortnightly Club. The Decum Club provided a social outlet for the men. It started in the home of Emile Smith and later moved to a room above a drug store on Main Street. A pool table was placed there for them. Dances were also sponsored and held by the club members. The original members were Emile Smith, Howard Ball, Sr., Tom Brown, and Noah Carlisle. Other members included Bill Bankhead, Ralph Trigg, Francis Ely, Kenneth Ellis, Jim Trotters, and Josh Campbell.

The Starlight Social Club was centered on the A.M.E. Church Choir and was a mix of young men and women. Their purpose was for social relaxation after choir practice. The members included Elise and Gene Newton, Alice and Ken Saunders, Wilbur Carlisle, Joan Moss (Carlisle), Martha Jackson, Dolores Carlisle, Janet and Carol Brown, and John Wesley Moss.

The Say and Do Club was formed about 1957 and disbanded about 1966. The purpose of the women's club was not only for social reasons, but also to provide assistance to the church. Two of their major projects were to replace the old gaslight fixtures downstairs with electric lights and to furnish the primary nursery section of the Sunday School room. The original members of this club were Dolores Carlisle, Alice Saunders, Joan Carlisle, Gladys Keels, Ruby Fisher, Mary Nichols, and Shirley Jones. The membership remained the same throughout the years with the later addition of Mary Jane Stewart Newman.

Mom was a member of the Say and Do Club. I remember being a small girl, and I laid across her bed to watch her get dressed to go to a meeting. I recall vividly when they had a special outing to Columbus to go to dinner at the Kahiki restaurant and to a movie to see *It is a Mad, Mad, Mad, Mad World*. She wore a turquoise dress with flowers on it, a white hat, and a pearl necklace. I thought she looked so beautiful. She had me laughing the next day with her tales of their evening out. I told Mom I could not wait until I grew up and graduated from high school so that I could be in the club with her. Unfortunately, I was six years too late.

The members of the Say and Do Club rotated meetings at the members' homes. My brothers and I loved it when it was Mom's turn. She always made homemade ginger bread with this wonderful lemon sauce. The aroma filled the house. We made sure that she made extras so we could finish eating what was left after the meeting.

The 1960s and 70s saw many social changes take place throughout Lancaster and the entire country in the wake of the Great Civil Rights Movement. The black citizens were no longer barred and segregated form public places. They were able to attend other churches and to attend community functions. In Lancaster, the younger generation was free to associate and socialize with white youth. As a result, they did not really see the need for the black clubs. As the members aged, the groups disbanded. Most of them dissolved in the mid to late 1960s. About the same time, membership of Allen Chapel A.M.E. Church dwindled, and the church underwent changes.

In 1981, the members of Allen Chapel legally withdrew from the A.M.E. denomination after the A.M.E. conference tried to take over the ownership of the church and the property. The court case was argued in the local courts and the Ohio State Supreme Court. The case was ultimately taken to the United States Supreme Court to settle this dispute.

Although many members left under protest in the 1960s, the black community as a whole supported the remaining members in their decision to withdraw from the A.M.E. conference. They were successful in winning their case and renamed the church Allen Chapel Independent Church.

The trustees appointed were Betty Grogans, Stanley "Buddy" Carlisle and Mary Ball.

Will Bennett eventually became minister of Allen Chapel. Under his pastorship in the mid-1980s, the church flourished and underwent a period of growth. Being a young man in his 30s, Bennett was able to draw a number of young adults and their families back to the church of their grandparents. There were enough members to have a choir once again. Several activities and church picnics were held at the church. It seemed that Allen Chapel was reaching out to the Lancaster community and would return to the activity level of its former days. Plans were made to clean and paint the church, and Bennett opened a building fund to which members made contributions. Many offers from various churches, community organizations, and individuals in Lancaster were made to remodel Allen Chapel at no cost to the congregation.

However, the trustees had other plans in mind. For reasons unknown to the congregation as a whole, the trustees and their family members repeatedly refused the generous offers. They did many things to discourage people from attending church services. They made rules, such as people could not sing in the choir unless they were recognized members. Continual disagreements developed between the older and younger members, particularly about the constantly changing rules of membership. Eventually, people became uncomfortable with the various situation and disputes that occurred during church services that they stopped coming. Bennett was replaced as minister by Donnie Evans of Columbus. In 1989, the trustees dismissed Evans and asked Bennett to return as pastor.

Bennett again made attempts to increase the membership of Allen Chapel and to remodel the church, again, to no avail.

On April 8, 1990, Palm Sunday, the church trustees unexpectedly announced the doors to Allen Chapel would be closed until further notice. Pastor Bennett and I were the only other people there besides the trustees, the church secretary, Phyllis Hawkins and their family members. They told Pastor Bennett to surrender his copy of the church key. They went on to say they were closing the church "indefinitely" and would notify Bennett when they reopened the church.

In February of 1991, an anonymous person called Alice Saunders and told her that if she were interested in keeping the church open, she better find out why the church and its property were being sold. When Mom found this to be true, she requested and successfully obtained an emergency court order to stop the sale.

In 1991, black and white citizens who believed the church had to be preserved for the black community, formed a committee headed by Mom. They went to court against the three trustees of Allen Chapel. Terre Vandervoort, who was fresh out of law school agreed to take the case and represented the concerned citizens.

Terre went to school with my brother, Evan, and are they are still good friends. She is a third generation of respected attorneys in Lancaster. Her father and grandfather were not sure Terre was ready for such a case, but Terre was determined to try it for us. Afterwards, her father admitted she learned more in this one case than she would have learned in ten years as a practicing attorney. A short time after the conclusion of the court case, Terre quickly rose to City Prosecutor, and she is still a strong supporter of the church.

Fairfield County Common Pleas Court Judge John Martin ordered the church to remain open and for regular church services to be held while the court heard the case. The judge said he expected to see a fair number of people attend the services as a testament that they were truly interested in keeping the church as a viable place of worship.

In 1993, the court ruled the church cannot be sold according to the quit-claim deed. This decision was upheld in the Ohio Supreme Court. The U.S. Supreme Curt refused to hear the case on the grounds that it was similar in nature to the 1981 case and, because of the quit-claim deed, the results of which would be the same--the church and its property cannot be sold.

On November 25, 1993, Judge Martin ruled that a three-member interim board would be appointed by the court for Allen Chapel. This board would have the responsibility of establishing a constitution, by-laws, and membership procedures for the church. Once a congregation was formed and a bookkeeping system was in place, as well as at least part-time ministerial supervision, the congregation would be asked to vote for a constitution, by-laws and a board of trustees. Judge Martin said, "In short, it is incumbent upon the court to see to it that this church becomes organized and functional." Judge Martin referred to a previous lawsuit involving Allen Chapel in 1983 in which he named three church members as the board of trustees for church. However, this board did not lead to the development and growth of the congregation. Over the course of time, the number of trustees dwindled down to one and no elections were conducted to replace the other two trustees. No constitution or by-laws were ever established as ordered by the court.

On December 6, 1983, Judge Martin appointed an interim board to assist the church to grow and flourish: Ron Keaton, president of Fairfield Federal Savings and Loan; Marlena Kane, owner of Hammonds Men's Store; and Jon Hall, an executive with Anchor Hocking Glass Corporation. The interim board was given the power to control and oversee the finances of the church during their term, which was "indefinite and until formally released by the court." Judge Martin stated the three interim trustees are individuals who "represent persons who are neighbors to the church, who are well established in the business community, who have vital legal and financial experience, and those who have valuable experience in arbitration and mediation." These individuals also demonstrated a history of long-standing community service and a willingness to volunteer and contribute to the betterment of this community.

The church was renamed Allen Chapel Church, and the interim trustees met many times in an effort to get the church back on track as quickly as possible. One of the first steps was to hire Rev. Joseph Yancy as the part-time minister of the church. Prior to this, Rev. Yancey was hired by Betty Grogans as pastor of Allen Chapel on an irregular basis in April 1991 until they dismissed him in November of the same year.

The excitement and hope were evident on the faces of those who attended Allen Chapel on the first Sunday of the church's re-opening, which was December 22, 1993. Rev. Yancey's sermon on that Sunday was appropriately titled, "A New Beginning." It was a service of celebration, filled with praise and thanksgiving, as the church was beautifully decorated for the Christmas season. Rev. Yancey expressed that "the church is a wonderful church with wonderful people who are in need of spiritual growth." He said the division of the church would not be resolved unless those involved are willing to let the healing begin. He saw his role as ministering the Word of God which is the only way to heal and bring about reconciliation. It was a disappointment that Betty Grogans and the other three members, including Francis "Sis" McKinley and Phyllis Hawkins, did not attend the services.

The three interim trustees of the church expressed confidence that the first service was truly a new beginning for Allen Chapel Church. They said they were excited to play a small role in helping to lay a new, firm foundation for the church but stressed the new congregation would be the builders. All were hopeful that not only would there be physical improvements of the church structure, but that there would be a renewal of Christian love and fellowship among the congregation of Allen Chapel and the community of Lancaster.

A board of trustees was eventually voted in by the congregation, and the court appointed trustees relinquished leadership of the church. These trustees were Alice Saunders, Valeria Hughes, and Joe Carlisle. Ron Keaton continues to be the church's financial advisor, however.

The Lancaster community once again supported the members of Allen Chapel. The building had fallen into disrepair. In the spring of 1994, attorneys, doctors, businessmen, and others donated time, money and materials to paint the church and to do basic remodeling. Even honor inmates from nearby Southeastern Correctional Institution assisted in the on-going work to restore the church building. The First United Methodist Church organized a group called Friends of Allen Chapel to offer continual support.

The members of Allen Chapel view the church, not only as a place to worship God, as a historical building with a rich heritage for the black community. They are also aware that the white community has played a large part by continuing to support the church in many different ways. The congregation, which consists of black and white members, stresses that the church is open to all people regardless of race, color, creed and social background.

Ministers who followed Pastor Yancey included Elder Herbert Smith, Elder Franklin, and Pastor Martin Tibbs. Deacon Evan Saunders is the current pastor of Allen Chapel.

In recent years, Allen Chapel has opened its doors to the community as a venue for the Lancaster Festival, Christmas Candlelight Tour, and Fairfield Heritage Association Tour of Historic Homes and Buildings, In the spring of 2005, the church also took part, along with South School and the Masonic Temple, in the Heritage Association's History Walk which featured Lancaster's black historical figures, including Emmanuel Carpenter and Scipio Smith, Scott James, Rev. John Viney, an escaped slave, Rube and Bertha Moss, and Emile Smith.

Allen Chapel also, on occasions, fellowships and have combined services with smaller predominantly white churches, including Good Shepherd Church and Pastor James Dexter, Joy Acres and Pastor Steve Rauch, Cross Pointe and Pastor Bill Pitts, and First Baptist Church, a black church in Nelsonville with Rev. Ronald Chunn.

Chapter 4

Black-owned Businesses Helped in the Growth of Lancaster

Black citizens of Lancaster and Fairfield County made a significant contribution to the business and professional community. When the ex-slaves and early settlers made their homes in Lancaster in as early as 1810, they either continued their trade or became apprentices and, in turn, established their own businesses.

Nelson Smith and his lineage were very popular in town. Nelson, who came to Lancaster from Virginia is the early 1800s, was a barber by trade and practiced for 50 years until his death in 1880. His barbershop was reportedly located on the east side of South Columbus Street, south of Walnut Street. His home was located at the corner of South Columbus and Winding streets. His home served as headquarters for the black people of Lancaster in the late 1840s. Many of the black residents gathered at Smith's barbershop to talk about politics and news of the day.

At midnight on July 31, 1848, the "rough element in town," which consisted of white people, badly damaged Nelson's home and destroyed most of the furniture. Despite the behavior of this mob, Nelson was reportedly regarded as the most noted "colored" man who ever lived in Lancaster. Nelson was proud of the fact that the noted attorney and political leader, Thomas Ewing, chose him to take care of Daniel Webster during Webster's two-week stay in Lancaster in 1833. It was said that Nelson was the favorite of the men of the old school who knew how to appreciate faithful and intelligent service.

Nelson passed this self-confidence and patronage of the people down to his children. He had several sons who succeeded him in the business. In fact, three continuous generations were barbers. They all lived in the block of Winding, Chestnut, and South Columbus streets. One son was Moses Redman Smith, born January 6, 1857. I was told that he had a barbershop in the old Mithof Hotel in the downtown area. Moses and his wife, Rebecca Anne Scott, had three sons, Oliver Moses, Ray Scott, and Emile Paul, who all followed in the family business.

Emile Smith was born on October 25, 1907 and worked at his shop located at 400 S. Columbus Street. I was told that Emile found an ingenious way to learn how to barber and make money doing so.

During his high school years, Emile was a caddy at the Lancaster Country Club and continued after he graduated. He also received a dollar a week from his father to clean and sweep his barbershop. According to the stories I heard, Emile practiced cutting hair by bargaining with the other caddies. He gave them free haircuts and, in exchange, they cleaned the shop. It is said that Emile still received pay from his father since his father assumed Emile cleaned the shop.

On January 28, 1934, Emile married Olive Margaret Weaver, a native of Circleville. In addition to his own barbershop, Emile was a bar manager at the Lancaster Country Club from 1946 to 1956. He was also bar manager at Shaw's Restaurant from 1956 to 1966.

Olive Smith owned and operated Smith's Catering service for 25 years until she retired in 1969. She then worked as a library assistant at Ohio University-Lancaster campus until 1975. She was in charge of all the periodicals. Olive served on the board of directors of the Lancaster YM-YWCA, and was a member of the Fortnightly Club. She was also noted to be the founder and den mother of the first integrated Boy Scout troop, which was reportedly sponsored by South Elementary School. On August 5, 1958, Olive was elected to serve on the board of directors of the Citizens Council for Better Schools.

Emile and Olive enjoyed many activities at Olivedale Senior Center and were active ballroom dancers. They had two children, Barbara Ann Smith Patrick and Daniel Paul Smith, an educator, who is now dean of students at Pickerington High School North. Danny said he could remember how Emile helped him build a racer for the soapbox derby in July of 1958, the first year that Danny participated in the derby. I do not think there were any other black youth who participated in the annual soapbox derby until Erin Hughes raced in 2002. Although she did not place, she was honored with the Rookie of the Year award. She raced again in 2004, the same year her brother, Quincy raced. He won 8th place in the regular stock division and was named Rookie of the Year. In 2006, their sister, Kenya, joined them as a soapbox derby participant.

Another well-known black-owned business was the Lancaster Transference and Storage Company, founded by Harry Rube Moss, who was born around 1893 to Harry T. and Ada Mae Moss. Rube Moss worked at the Kirn Building shining shoes. He also was said to have operated a cigar and tobacco parlor. He later began to haul trunks and luggage from the train depot located on Porter Street on the south-end to the various hotels in the downtown area. Eventually he was very much in demand. In 1916, Rube opened a building at the rear of 408 E. Mulberry Street. In 1921, he opened an office in the front of the building and a garage in 1927.

Widely known as a man of his word, Rube brought his business successfully through the Depression. He freed many people of their unpaid bills, especially if he knew they could not pay anything. He was in the Dunn & Bradstreet Listings. Rube boasted of having unlimited credit and was able to claim a spotless credit record.

The Lancaster Transference and Storage Company were granted an intrastate license to allow Rube to transport freight and household goods within the State of Ohio. Later, the business received an Interstate license and traveled independently in seven states: Illinois, Indiana, West Virginia, Pennsylvania, New York, and New Jersey. The seventh state was either Kentucky or Virginia, and I do not know the dates these licenses were granted.

Rube was also contracted with the United States Armed Forces during World War II to do crating and shipping. After the war, they did crating and shipping of heavy commercial equipment for various industries. The company was the only one that moved safes. One of the company's last jobs was to deliver the big safe to the *Lancaster Eagle-Gazette*.

It was reported that during the height of the successful business, Moss had three trucks and six men on staff. Five of these men were Ralph Smith, Walter Moxley, Rollie Fisher, Albert Jones, and Clark Wolfe. The sixth man could not be identified.

In addition to the Lancaster Transference and Storage Company, it was said that Rube was one of the first exterminators in Lancaster.

Rube met and, in 1906, married Bertha Flowers Muntz, who was from Waverly, Ohio. She came to Lancaster as a licensed beauty operator and lived with George and Fern Anderson. Bertha was in business for about 30 years. Her salon, located at 408 E. Mulberry Street was one of the largest beauty salons in town and catered to the wealthy and prominent citizens of Lancaster. The Mosses had one child, Joan Mae Moss, who was married to Wilbur H. Carlisle and lived at 412 E. Mulberry Street.

In addition to his business, Rube was involved in the community in various ways through the years. In May of 1916, Rube captained the Lancaster Blues baseball team. The other players of the team consisted of George Anderson, Earl Hunster, Charles Byrd, James Byrd, William Allen, Oscar Hawkins, Ralph Hawkins, Henry Hawkins, Walter Smith, and Walter Randall. George Anderson was elected president and manager of the team, and Earl Hunter was named treasurer and James Byrd was secretary of the team. People who wanted to play games against the Lancaster Blues went to George Anderson at the Mithoff Barbershop or to Rube Moss at the Kirn Building lobby. The team expected to put Lancaster on the baseball map and was willing to change their name to that of any local businessman who sponsored them.

Rube was also involved with the Shriners. On July 21, 1927, Rube, along with Dr. J.E. Gray and George Bibbs, served on a committee that brought 100 members of the Mystic Shrine of Alla Baba Temple in Columbus for a parade and concert in the City Hall Park in Lancaster. Following the concert, lodge members and their friends assembled at the Sherman Amory for a social program, dancing and refreshments.

Around 1952, Bertha took over the storage company due to the illness of Rube, who eventually died on September 30, 1959. Bertha sold the business to Earl Holliday and the Chieftain Express in 1968. I remember the black community came together and helped Joan and Wilbur with the sale and auction of business-related items.

Bertha died several months later of cancer. The warehouse located at the rear of 408 E. Mulberry Street burned down in 1975. Sadly, many historical papers and pictures pertaining to the highly regarded business were destroyed.

The Tibbs family was another successful and hard-working family in Lancaster and Fairfield County. Qualles Tibbs owned and operated a truck farm or produce garden on his eleven and a half-acre farm located at 1271 S. Broad Street sometime in the mid to latter 1800's. Qualles and his two sons, Sheridan and Albert, furnished vegetables for the city of Lancaster, and deliveries were made on Tuesdays, Thursdays, and Fridays.

Before he settled down on his farm, Qualles served in the Civil War as fifth sergeant of Company E, 27th Regiment during the Civil War. Upon his return to Lancaster, Qualles was an active member of the Allen Chapel A.M.E. Church and the G.A.R. Post. He devoted the greater part of his life to gardening,

Qualles died in 1922 at the age of 86, and, up to the time of his death, was Lancaster's oldest resident. He left behind 10 children, 15 grandchildren, and 6 great-great children.

Fred Tibbs reportedly owned the first barbershop in Carroll, Ohio. He moved to Lancaster in the early 1900s. Fred opened his barbershop on Maple Street and later moved it to Broad Street on the current site of the Lancaster Police Department. His two sons, Herbert and Ernest, worked for him. It has been said that Fred provided his customers with more than haircuts and shaves. His shop also included tubs for hot baths.

Clifford Tibbs worked at the Alcohol Treatment Center in the early 1920s. He was said to be either valedictorian or salutatorian of his graduating high school class. Clifford died in 1924 of tuberculosis.

Norman Tibbs, Sr. lived in Steubenville as a youth. While living there, he sold newspapers at the age of nine and had his own corner. At the age of 12, he became an apprentice barber, and at the age of 15 became a full-fledged barber. Norman returned to Lancaster in 1930 and completed his high school education in 1932.

Norman told me that he worked for the Lancaster Post Office for many years. From 1934 to 1959, he worked as a mail carrier. He then worked inside as a postal clerk until his retirement on June 20, 1973.

Pearl Anderson, as I understand it, had the oldest shoeshine business in Lancaster, which was more than 40 years. He had the friendship and respect of many people in Lancaster, including the town's leading citizens.

Pearl learned to shine shows while he was in the sixth grade. He first worked after school and on Saturdays in the shoeshine parlor located in the Martens Building, located in the Public Square at 1 North Broad Street. After graduating from Lancaster High school in 1910, Pearl continued to work in the shop and later became its owner. In 1938, Anchor Hocking remodeled the building and turned it into office space. Pearl moved his shoe shine business to the Equitable Building, home of the Equitable Savings and Loan Company, now Bank One.

No matter where his business was located, it is said that Pearl possessed personal qualities that distinguished him. People said that Pearl always had a cheerful disposition, which raised the spirits of many customers and had great pride in doing a good job. Pearl and his wife, Nelly, made their home at 424 E. Mulberry Street.

There were a number of black residents who were respected for their profession or trade.

Tom "T.B." Brown operated his shoeshine parlor inside the Equitable Building downtown until his death in 1961. Tom learned his trade by working with Pearl Anderson

Tom raised his family on East Locust Street. I remember seeing him walk to work every morning, smiling and waving to people as they passed. When Pearl died in 1946, Tom took over the business. Tom was also a custodian at the Equitable Building from 1952 until his death.

Tom's wife, Malva, was also well loved throughout the Lancaster community. Malva graduated in 1930 from Central State University in Xenia under their two-year program in education. She had a dream of becoming a teacher, but at that time, black people could only find teaching jobs in the southern states. I was told that her father refused to permit her to leave to go South. Instead, she moved to Lancaster, met and married Tom Brown and put her dreams aside to raise her three children, Carol, Janet and Greg, and later her grandson, Mark Jones.

As a fantastic cook, Malva used her talent and her college training by working for many years as a head cook in the school cafeterias at South School and Stanbery Junior High School. The students loved her, loved her fantastic homemade food, and affectionately called her "Ma Brown." I remember sitting in study hall in the cafeteria the period before lunch, trying to ignore the mouth-watering aromas and the scent of peanut butter and oatmeal cookies being baked. Malva was also an assistant to Olive Smith in the Smith's Catering Services.

Malva's dream of teaching finally became reality when the Head Start Program came to Fairfield County. She was given the opportunity to take a refresher course in education and assume the position of director of the Lancaster program. Everyone who knew Malva was well aware of her devotion to the children and to the Head Start program. She later reluctantly retired from this position due to the arthritic conditions of her knees. Sadly, she developed Alzheimer's disease and required placement in a nursing home in Columbus for several years before she died. Malva will always be remembered by those who came in contact with her for her quick smile and witty remarks.

Noah and Mary Martha Carlisle lived their married life on East Locust Street. Noah worked at Gallagher's Drug Store and later at Stewart Brothers and Alban Company. Mary ran the elevator at the old Kirn Building.

John Harris, Sunday School superintendent of the Allen Chapel A.M.E. Church and deacon of the church made his home on East Wheeling Street. His daughter, Jessie Harris Ball married and moved to Mulberry Street and was said to have been a sales clerk at Wiseman's Clothing Store.

Charles "Chalk" Hunster was a well-known masseur and, up to the mid-1930s, owned a parlor located on South Columbus Street, next door to what is now W.G. Grinders. He was also a barber. I was also told that Charles was an excellent musician who formed a string quartet with other musicians, his brother Earl, Okley Byrd, and George Anderson. They performed for many parties and dances in and around Lancaster. Charles' home was located on Lawrence Street. His brother, Earl Hunster, lived on Maple Street and operated a shoeshine parlor in City Hall.

Another local musician during this time was Ike Freeman. He was well known as a one-man band, not only in Lancaster, but also around the state of Ohio. Ike had instruments rigged together so that he could play the "juice harp" or the harmonica, cymbals, a big bass drum, and guitar at the same time. Ike played at most of the county fairs. He reportedly was paid when people dropped money into his cup while he played. He also competed in various contests. I was told that one year, Ike won the state championship and was asked to represented Ohio in the national contest that was held in Columbus. However, a few days prior to the contest, Ike caught pneumonia and died.

Several people recalled ice-skating on the old canal bed during the early 1900s. It was said that Bill Hooper was the best skater in town. He reportedly was so good that he was able to draw a man's head on the ice while skating.

Jennie Mary Streets Hawkins is a name that people remembered with fondness. She was married to Frank Hawkins, Sr., who was a janitor for many years at the Goodman's Shoe Factory. They made their home at 338 E. Locust Street, then on Allen Street, and they finally settled on a large farm on Rainbow Drive. The Hawkins Farm was often the setting of many picnics for their relatives and friends.

Many people who knew Jennie Mary called her Aunt Jen. Everyone agreed she was an excellent cook. Especially remembered were her famous apple pies. People said her crust was so flaky and light they ate more of it than the filling.

I remember a little bit about Aunt Jen, who died in 1974 at the age of 102, two years after I graduated from Lancaster High School. While I was in junior high school, I remember after church, Dad would sometimes drive us to the farm. Her kitchen smelled good, as she and the family prepared Sunday dinner. I recalled she was always laughing and talking about days gone by. I only wish I could remember the many stories she told. Aunt Jen and Frank raised a family of eight children: Ellen, Frank, Jr., Oscar, Ralph, Anna, Star, John, and Paul.

The Hawkins kids were considered to be "the sports family of the 1930s." The boys mostly played on the football team at Lancaster High School. Paul was a 3-letterman in football, baseball, and basketball. Oscar passed his athletic abilities to his son, Oscar, Jr. who was the talk of the town in 1936 when he ran 98 yards for the winning touchdown against Zanesville with a few seconds left in the game.

Oscar Hawkins and his wife, Lulu, lived on Wheat Street, moved to Wheeling Street, and then settled at the corner of Maple and Locust streets. Lulu was a domestic worker for a local wealthy family while Oscar was a househusband. I was told that he was an excellent housekeeper and cook. He reportedly shared his household hints and recipes with others. Lulu was active at Allen Chapel and was good at making decorative items. I remember how she took a bar of soap and put pretty pictures on the soap to make it decorative.

In their later years, they often sat on the front porch of their home that faced Maple Street. They waved at people who passed by. I enjoyed stopping by and talking with Lulu whenever I saw her out.

When Oscar and Lulu's daughter, Becky married Arthur Gooden in the 1940s at Allen Chapel, the wedding was considered to be "the" social event. Many local blacks attended and recalled that everyone had a wonderful time. George L. Hawkins worked for the Lancaster Building Supply Company. He was said to have started his own garbage collection business in 1936 until his death in 1941.

Other black residents who reportedly operated their own business as garbage collectors in the early 1920s included George Ford, John Harris, Earl Jenkins, and Harry Strouder.

Susie Carter, the first and oldest practicing chiropodist in Lancaster, lived most of her life on Mulberry Street and practiced from an office on South Columbus Street. I was told that Susie learned her profession from a Dr. Carey in Cincinnati, following her graduation from Lancaster High school.

Phyllis Hawkins was noted to be one of the two first meter maids in Lancaster. She was appointed by the City Council on July 28, 1958. Phyllis was also active at Allen Chapel A.M.E. Church, and played piano for church for several years. She lived on East Mulberry Street.

In the early years of Lancaster, Alex Cunningham owned the city's livery stables, which were located at Chestnut and Columbus streets. The stables were later converted to the Central Delivery. From there, horse and wagons made deliveries to merchants all over town. Alex was married to the daughter of Nelson Smith.

I was told that there were other independent black workers who provided their services to the Lancaster community. Several families who hauled garbage and trash were known as "honey-dippers," another name for people who took care of outhouses. In addition there were truck gardeners, people who raised produce and sold them from their trucks.

As Lancaster moved into the 1940s and beyond, the number of black-owned businesses declined noticeably. More and more members of the community found employment in the domestic service area, being employed by some of the prominent white families and establishments in town.

Chapter 5

Discrimination in Lancaster

Black residents living in Lancaster have always been few in numbers, making up less than two percent of the total population. Prior to the 1970s, the majority of black families lived on Locust, Maple and Walnut streets on the south-end, and Wheeling and Mulberry streets on the east side. A few families were scattered around town and in the country.

Buying houses in other parts of the city was almost unheard of and was difficult to do unless a potential home owner who was black was sponsored by a prominent white resident. Today, blacks can buy a house pretty much wherever they want to live as long as they can afford it. Because of this, unlike many towns and cities, there is no large concentration of blacks in any one part of Lancaster.

Dad recalled that he grew up in an apartment complex known as the Red Onion. He said there were about 20 families, both black and white, who all were on welfare. He said there were about 50 kids who lived there, and they all played together with little or no problems. In the summer, the families often had cookouts and all the families would bring something to eat to share with everyone. He said while there was obvious segregation in Lancaster, there was also a line drawn according to where you lived, which may have been stronger than your skin color. There was an unstated east-side versus west-side mentality that still exists today.

In the early years of Lancaster, blacks owned a variety of businesses, from blacksmithing, produce stores, and other establishments which will be addressed later in this book. For whatever reason, most of these black-owned businesses dwindled and disappeared. Many of the black residents, instead, were in the employment of wealthy and prominent white citizens. Several of the families who employed blacks were I.J. Collins, William Fisher and Phillip Rising. The blacks were chauffeurs, cooks, maids, butlers, and gardeners in these homes, while others did laundry and ironing in their own homes. Only a few, including my dad, worked outside of homes and in factories. The white families treated their black help with respect and dignity, according to what I was told by those employed by the wealthy families. My grandmother worked for the Risings and had no problems. I was told that a wife of one of a prominent business man asked a guest to leave her home when the guest referred to one of the black help as a "nigger maid." Some of the families made sure the blacks were adequately provided for after they left their employment.

I've already talked a little about how blacks were not permitted to socialize with the whites. There were other racist barriers to prevent equal treatment in town. My dad told me stories about how the blacks were not allowed to swim in the public swimming pool at Miller Park. Dad said the only time they could swim was on Fridays because the pool was drained and cleaned on Friday nights and filled with fresh water. He also told us that they had a way of getting back that went undetected. He said a group of young blacks, sometimes with several white friends, after they knew the pool was refilled, would often sneak out very late on Friday night and swim in the fresh, clean water. They were never caught doing this. The black youth in the mid '60s and 70s swam at Miller Pool without much incident. We had no trouble getting in, but there were some people who did not like it. We had too much fun to let those few people bother us. We learned to stay together, keep a low profile and not draw attention to ourselves, and to ignore anyone who tried to bother us because of our race. We preferred to go to Tiki Pools on Sheridan Drive, but at that time, blacks were not welcomed in that part of Lancaster. This changed in the late '70s and '80s, and the pool was opened to everyone.

The Klu Klux Klan made their presence known in Lancaster. From what I was told, the Klan did not cause any problems for the black residents, such as was being done in the South. I talked with several older local residents, both black and white, and they remembered a parade of sorts was held by Klan members in 1927. They said they could recall a large number of Klan people, complete with robes and white hoods, marched down Main Street to Broad Street to the Fairgrounds. They said it was a rather peaceful march, although it was disturbing and scary to see, regardless of race.

I was also told that, in the late 1930s, a large group of KKK members gathered on top of Mount Pleasant where a mass wedding and a cross burning took place. To my knowledge, this was the only incident of cross burning that took place in Lancaster. However, in the nearby village of Baltimore, a cross was burned on the front lawn of a man who had bi-racial grandchildren. This incident took place in April 2006.

I cannot remember exactly the year, but sometime in the early 1990's a surge of KKK rallies seem to sweep across Ohio. Cincinnati was one of the larger cities where scenes of rioting and protesting of Klan rallies. Residents of Lancaster were informed that a leader of an Ohio clan had asked for a permit to hold a rally on the steps of City Hall. I recall that both white and black residents protested and urged the mayor not to grant the permit. The mayor said that he had to be fair and allow the permit to go through. There was much discussion in town about what people should do. The church community came forward as a leader in this situation and urged people not to attend the rally, but instead meet at the downtown gazebo for prayer during the rally. The black community urged black residents to stay clear of the rally and not to feed into the Klan's' beliefs. Several community-wide prayer vigils were held prior to the appointed day of the rally. And God in his wisdom heard those prayers. The rally was not held because the leader was arrested for domestic violence against his wife, and the Klan cancelled the rally.

Lancaster's downtown area, at one time, was the main area for shopping, businesses, entertainment, and just meeting and talking with others. Downtown used to be vibrant and thriving, a place to go, especially on Friday night and on Saturdays. For the most part, black citizens could shop and do business with little or no problems. However, before the Civil Rights Movement, there were places that discouraged blacks. There were some stores and restaurants that had "No Coloreds Allowed" signs in their windows during the 1940s. A few restaurants would only serve blacks if they went to the back where the kitchen was and ordered food to be taken home.

Steve Carlisle said he recalled when he was about five years old, which would be about 1958; he went to the courthouse with his grandmother, Bertha Moss. He said he had to go to the restroom, and remembered his grandmother told him he could not because there was a "Whites Only" sign on the door.

White Cottage, then located on North high Street, close to Sixth Avenue, was one such place that did not allow blacks to enter their establishment to eat.

Dad recalled an incident while he was in high school in the 1940s. He was on the Lancaster High School football team, and he said sometimes the players used to stop in at White Cottage to grab something to eat. Dad said one day he went into the restaurant to get a sandwich when a lady behind the counter asked him what he was doing there and said that he was not supposed to be in there. She did give him the hamburger he ordered, and he left, but he could not eat it. He has never set foot inside the restaurant since then.

This policy with White Cottage was still true in the mid-1960s. My brothers and I always knew that blacks were not permitted to go into White Cottage, even to order food for carry-out. Many times my friends and I walked by the restaurant when we went to the fairgrounds during the county fair or to Rising Park. I always wondered what their famous hamburgers tasted like. The aroma that drifted from White Cottage only whetted my curiosity to taste one. One day, I could no longer resist.

A group of us were returning home after spending a day at the county fair. When we walked by White Cottage, I asked Kenny and Lawrence what would happen if I went in to buy a hamburger. They told me that I was not supposed to go in. Debby Clagg said if I wanted one, she would go in and buy one.

When she went in, I slipped in after her. I was also curious as to what it looked like inside. I remember that everyone inside noticed me; they stopped talking and eating. The lady at the counter asked me what did I want, and I said a hamburger. She told me that I was not permitted to be in there, so I asked her why. She did not have an answer. She did say that if I did not leave, she would call the police. I said okay and told Debby that I did not want the sandwich and left.

Carrie Hacker and her mother bought the restaurant from the original owners in 1976. The new owners did not tolerate any type of discrimination in the restaurant. The small building burned down in 1999. Carrie reopened the restaurant in the downtown area in 2001. When I interviewed Carrie as part of an assignment for the *Lancaster Eagle-Gazette*, I was able to finally taste a famous White Cottage hamburger.

As I was saying, I can remember the problems I had as a young girl growing up in the 1960s and early 70s. Kenny, Lawrence, and I liked to go downtown with our white friends and neighbors: Tony, Debbie and Nicky Clagg, Jimmy King, and sometimes Sonny Johnson. We went to Kresge's "five and dime store" on Fountain Square, which was where the Lancaster City School Education Service Center was housed until it was sold in 2006. We liked to go back to the toy section to look at the comic books. We wandered through the store, went to the candy section that dominated the middle of the store, and usually ended up at the luncheon counter to buy soda pop or ice cream. My brothers and I were almost always followed around the store by a store employee, as if we would steal something. If we picked up an item and looked at it, the employee sometimes asked us if we had the money to buy it. I recall seeing white kids shoplifting and getting by with it because the employee was too busy following us around. When we went to the counter to buy something to drink or eat, only our white friends could sit at the counter. My brothers and I had to stand behind the seats, or preferably, take it out of the store with us. Some years later when I was a young teen, we could sit in the last five seats at the far end of the counter. It was not until the early 1970s that we could sit anywhere we wanted.

Kenny's Restaurant, at the corner of Main and Columbus streets, was another place that did not serve blacks. One time in the late 1960s, I went to Kenny's with Debbie Clagg and Charlene King. The waitress came to our table and took Debbie's and Charlene's order and left. Debbie called her back and said she forgot to take my order. She gave me a dirty look and said that she did not serve "her kind." Both

Debbie and Charlene said I was just as good as anyone else and should be able to eat there. The waitress said I really had no right to be there. The two girls got up and said they would not give their money to such a place, and we left.

Most businesses and business owners did not care about the skin color of their customers, as long as they were good customers. An example that comes readily to mind is Risch's Drug Store. Stanley Risch was fair with everyone. My parents have gone to the drug store located at the corned of Main and Maple streets for as long as I can remember. We still continue to be customers at the store, which is now operated by his son, Alan.

Whenever I walk into Risch's, I remember when my brothers and I, along with our friends liked to walk over there and see what toys and model car kits were in. We would also look at the magazines and buy candy. Often times we pulled our money together and bought ice cream and milk shakes at the lunch counter. Sometimes we stopped in after school since it was on the way home from Stanbery Junior High.

Since St. Mary Elementary School and Bishop Fenwick Catholic High School (now William V. Fisher Catholic High School) were located near Risch's, the Catholic students considered the store to be their hangout and were somewhat territorial of the lunch counter. Some of the students harassed us if we tried to sit at the counter. In order to avoid any fights, we would go on about our business. I remember one day several black students, myself included, were sitting at the counter, eating ice cream and talking when several Catholic students walked in. They walked up to us and demanded our seats, although there were other empty stools. We refused, and they said that "our kind" did not belong there anyway. Stanley Risch went over to the counter and very sternly said that he would not tolerate any foolishness and that everyone was welcomed to eat at the counter as long as they had the money. I do not recall any further problems at the store after that incident. However, we did have to fight our way to school when we went to Stanbery Junior High School if we were not able to outrun any Catholic students we encountered.

Despite these problems and incidents, the blacks were fortunate not to experience racial problems on the scale of other cities. But, I cannot minimize the problems that we faced. Prior to the 1970s and 80s, little opportunities were provided for blacks who had much to offer to their community. They were discouraged from teaching, hold any type of leadership positions in jobs, and to hold public offices or to be on any community boards. There were no black police, sheriff deputies, or firemen. In fact, the only black police officer to ever be on the Lancaster force was Scott James, who was on the force for less than a year in 1880.

Let me take a moment to explain who Scott James was and what happened to him. This is an example of what blacks have had to endure from a small population of whites in Lancaster. Scott was born as a slave sometime between 1842 and 1844 in either Alabama, Tennessee or Kentucky. After President Abraham Lincoln freed the slaves through the Emancipation Proclamation in 1863, Scott enlisted in the 15th regiment of the U.S. Colored Infantry and was mustered in Nashville, Tennessee. According to information by Dwight Barnes, historian with the *Lancaster*

Eagle-Gazette, Scott was eventually promoted to sergeant and was honorably discharged in 1866.

Scott came to Lancaster sometime before 1870 and lived in the home of Mrs. Ellen Qualls, who helped him to obtain a job in the brick yard and introduced him to Nelson Smith, who was a prominent black citizen in Lancaster. He met and married his wife, Anna. They eventually owned the first house built on East Walnut Street at 529 E. Walnut Street. Despite being unable to read or write, Scott quickly gained a reputation as being a hard worker and for being honest and straight-forward man.

After the sudden death of Policeman Levi Freisner on August 14, 1880, members of the City Council needed to find someone the majority of the council could agree on to fill the vacancy (at that time, policemen were appointed by the City Council at their discretion and not hired based on their qualifications as they are today). At that time the council was controlled by Democrats (six members were Democrats), who for the most part supported the South in the Civil War. According the information by Dwight Barnes, Councilman Tarpy wanted to get his brother-in-law, John Morris reinstated back on the police force. Morris reportedly was fired for neglect of duty. However, Scott James and a George East were nominated, and Scott was elected by a vote of 7-3 (three Democrats and four Republicans).

Shortly after he was hired, several charges were filed against Scott. One charge, neglect of duty, came down from Chief of Police Sol Nisley in December of 1880 after Scott, who was on night duty, reportedly went into the mayor's office to warm himself during his break. The charge was found to be groundless, following an investigation led by

Councilman George Beck and by Mayor William Vorys. It had been a longtime practice for all city police officers to take their breaks during duty hours in the mayor's office.

The other charge was actually because of an Officer James McFadden, who was told to serve an arrest warrant; however, he refused to serve the warrant if Scott accompanied him. He reportedly said his life and liberty would be at stake if Scott went with him. After several hearings, McFadden, who was charged with failure to carry out an assigned duty, was reprimanded and retained on the police force. Councilman Beck submitted the minority report in which he stated that the allegations had not been substantiated and that a number of charges had been disproved. However, Councilman Tarpy's majority report found Scott to be guilty.

According to information researched by Deward Watts and expressed in his historical reenactment, Tarpy recommended that the *"nagur b cashiered, dsimissed, turned out, ousted, boted, fired, set down upon, pulverized, scooped, cremated, eradicated, exterminated, extirpated, obliterated and eliminated from the police force, now then, henceforth, and forever [sic]!"*

Despite Council President Sites' strong argument to reprimand Scott but keep him on the force, the Council voted along party lines, 6 to 4, to remove him from the police force in the early part of 1881.

Scott worked as a laborer at the Eagle Iron Works factory after he was released from the police force. He remained active at the Allen Chapel A.M.E. Church where he eventually became a trustee. On July 30, 1880, Scott and Anna hosted a fete to benefit the church. It reportedly was well attended and raised a large sum of money for the church. According to information by Deward Watts, Scott was a member of the Garfield and Arthur Club, a Republican club for the black citizens. The sole purpose of the club was to get James Garfield and Chester Arthur elected President and Vice-President of the United States. Scott also was the first black man to serve on a jury in Lancaster.

Scott died on November 30, 1900 ten days after he contracted pneumonia while attending the funeral of Mrs. Qualles Tibbs.

There have been no other black police officers on the Lancaster police force since then in spite of several black applicants in the 1980s and 1990s. There are black law enforcement personnel working for the Fairfield County Sheriff's Office and the Lancaster Post of the Ohio State Highway Patrol, with Lt. Gary Lewis being the second black commander of the Lancaster Post.

The Civil Rights Movement touched the hearts of the blacks, not only in Lancaster, but also across the country. The Movement gave blacks a new sense of pride, a new awareness of how they were being treated because of their darker skin color and a new desire to learn about the contributions of their race and to make their own mark on the world.

One local couple was able to witness firsthand the famous "I Have a Dream" speech by Martin Luther King, Jr. in Washington D.C. in 1963. Betty Grogans recalled that she and her husband Grant Grogans went to Columbus and rode on one of a number of buses that caravanned to

Washington D.C. She said hundreds of people left from the Columbus area. Once in Washington, they joined thousands of people from all over the country to attend the rally. It was a very hot day, but the mood of the people was hopeful and inspired by the words of Dr. King. Betty said it was hard to describe what it was like that day, but that she returned to Lancaster with a renewed spirit

Racism and segregation were very familiar to both of the Grogans. Born in Marietta, Georgia, Grant was a musician who played the saxophone. He came to Lancaster and married Betty in 1952. Betty, born in 1925, was the youngest child of William and Bessie Allen. Betty said she recalled many incidents of segregation and that it was difficult for blacks to do anything. She said she remembered working for a white family while she was a student in high school, but did not stay for very long. Betty recalled that one day the lady of the house wanted her to wash out the toilets with her hands; she refused, and she did not go back.

The assassination of Dr. Martin Luther King, Jr. on April 4, 1968 threatened to stop the fight for equality in its track. It is a day that will forever live in my mind. That day was my youngest brother, Evan's 4th birthday. The family was in the kitchen celebrating with cake and ice cream and presents. My Dad asked me to go into the front room to get more light bulbs for the camera to take pictures. I walked by the television when the news bulletin came on. I forgot about the bulbs as I listened to the news about King's death. I yelled for Dad to come to the middle room, that King had been shot. Everyone else came in and watched.

Shortly after that, our phone started to ring constantly. A number of people came over to discuss what we should do, especially since news of riots in big cities was starting to trickle in. The adults decided it would be best that they go to work as usual and the kids go to school. We were told to go to school, keep a low profile and not to talk about King's assassination. The adults said they would contact the school principals and would make arrangements for us to miss school to stay home on the day of the funeral.

The next day, I went to Stanbery Junior High where I was an 8th grade student. Two of the black students who preferred to be into the Black Power Movement did not heed the words of the adults. They went to school wearing black clothes and a black armband. They went down the hallway at the end of a class period with raised fists and yelled "Black Power, Power to the People." I came out of science class and entered mass chaos. I remember being grabbed by a big 9th grade boy, and was slammed against the lockers. He spat in my face and said, "We killed one nigger, and we can kill some more." I was terrified.

I was looking around for my brother and saw all hell break loose. The hallway was filled with students shouting and pushing, some of the black students were being hit by whites as they fought, and teachers trying to regain control. Several of my friends, helped me get away from the white boy before I was hurt too badly and formed a circle around me to protect me. The teachers and principal rounded up the black students and put us into the auditorium. Several parents and the police came to the school and escorted us out of the building and home.

That evening, most of the black adults and families met at my parents' home. I cannot remember too much of what was said, but I do remember that the two boys who wore black to school were in trouble with the adults. We did not return to school and stayed close to home until after the funeral, which was televised on national television.

There was a feeling of unrest everywhere and Lancaster was no different. I recall going to Kresge's a few days after King's assassination to get some sewing material for Mom. I went in the back door where the sewing section was so I could get what I needed, check out at the back station, and leave without being really noticed. Two older white ladies were also looking at material and I overheard them talk about King's death and the rioting taking place in areas of the country. One lady said to the other, "I think it is just awful that Dr. King was killed. There is trouble in so many places. Do you think our coloreds will cause any trouble?" The other lady responded by saying, "I do not think so. Our coloreds know their place and would not cause any problems."

I remember feeling angry and wanted to say something. However, I quickly realized that they were raised in a different time and era, and they were right. I knew that change was in the air and that the blacks had to carry on with what King started. Too many people, both black and white, shed their blood, were imprisoned, and were beaten for us not to pick up the torch of racial equality and social justice. I resolved within my spirit to get as much education as I could and to help bring changes to Lancaster in a legal, ethical, moral and Christian manner.

It was about this time, as I said above, that I can look back and see how things changed, at least for me. Before the assassinations of King, Malcolm X, and Robert Kennedy, the Watts riots, and the Black Panthers and the Black Power

Movement, everything seemed so simple. I lived in a mixed neighborhood, with blacks, whites, Catholics, Protestants, and no one seemed to pay attention to our differences. Most of our neighbors were, and still are, close friends who looked out for each other. It was nothing for one of us to need something like an egg while baking, and if a neighbor was not home, go in, get an egg and leave a note. Many of the neighbor kids, black and white, played in our backyard. Granted, we had the most kids in our family and Mom was always home while Dad worked at Rockwell International, but everyone liked to come to our house. No one was turned away as long as they obeyed the house rules and behaved themselves. If they did not, they were banished from the yard for a set amount of time, which was a real punishment for them. Dad was known as the neighborhood "doctor" because everyone went to him with their bumps, bruises, cuts and scrapes, and he would clean and bandage any wounds. All the kids knew that if their bicycles or roller skates needed to be fixed, they could take them to Dad, and he would repair them. Mom and Dad listened to everyone's problems and sometimes loaned a tie or jewelry to one of the teens for a special date.

Minnie and her daughter, Jeannie Azbell were part of the largest white family on Locust Street. They have lived on Locust Street since 1952, three years before my family moved into the neighborhood, which had been racially mixed for many years. The Azbells agreed that color had never been an issue. They regarded the black families as friends and never thought about who was black or white. Minnie said through the years, they have all learned to rely on one another, keep an eye out for each other, and to help whoever was in need. Jeannie said it was the character of a person that counts, not skin color. She and her mother expressed affection and admiration for the blacks who lived on the street.

In addition to my parents, they described Albert and Ty Jones as a wonderful and friendly couple. Albert, affectionately referred to as "Jonesy" by everyone, always seemed to have time to wave as he drove by or stopped for a chat. One of his favorite hangouts was Baskins and Robbins ice cream parlor, then located on Sixth Avenue and Memorial Drive. "Jonesy" was one of those people who knew no strangers. Both Albert and Ty were employed by William V. Fisher for many years.

The other black families who lived on Locust Street included Stanley and Mary Turner and their children; Eddie and Margaret Jenkins, and their children; Minnie Saunders (my grandmother) and her son, (Uncle) Jim Saunders; Tom and Malva Brown and their children; Henry and Bonnie Hall and their children; and Walter and Ruby Moxley and their children.

As a young girl, our core neighborhood "gang" included my brothers, Kenny and Lawrence, myself (black), and Debby and Nick Clagg, Jimmy King, and Sonny Johnson (all white). We did almost everything together. During the summer, we got together in the morning after breakfast, took a break at lunch and dinner, and resumed our activities as far into the night as we could until our parents called us into the house. Sometimes we slept outside under makeshift tents or slept on the back porch of one of our houses. Debbie and I were like sisters and even liked to dress alike, but in different colors. We used to yell out our back windows to each other to see what was going on with each other.

When I was very little, when we first moved from the A.M.E. church parsonage to our Locust Street house, I can vaguely remember going out into the backyard with Kenny and Lawrence and looking at Debby, Nicky and Tony, and we all became fast friends. We spent summers playing baseball at South School or in the alley in between the Lancaster Farm store and the recycling place. We always went to craft days at Elmwood Park. One night a week, parents took turns popping bags of popcorn and filling a thermos of Kool-Aid for us to snack on during the outdoor movies at the park.

Many nights and days were spent playing tag, Mother May I, hide and seek, hopscotch, jacks, Seven-up, and jump rope. We also looked for worms, fished at Silver Lake, or just plain hung out and talked, and made up stories to scare each other.

Over time, other black kids, including David Moxley, Sammy Nichols, Mark Jones, Juan and Darryl Franklin, and the McKinleys joined our circle. The McKinleys were a large family, with about 12 kids in the family, who moved down the street from us when I was in junior high school. They were from Cincinnati, if I remember correctly, so they brought something different to our small town neighborhood. We got along well, for the most part. The family invited us to regular house dances, which were fun and exciting because it made me look at boys in a whole different light, instead of seeing them as just buddies.

I can still clearly remember one summer that changed everything for us in the neighborhood. It was either the summer of 1966 or 1967; the McKinleys had a cousin from Cincinnati who stayed with them for several months. I can still see our core gang and a few others standing under the big maple tree in front of our house, talking and laughing. We noticed the McKinley's station wagon coming over the hill and then it stopped. This teenaged boy with a large Afro hairstyle jumped out of the car, and with a raised fist, ran down the street yelling "Black Power. Power to the people" at the top of his voice. We looked at him and wondered what the heck he was doing.

In the following weeks, we tried to be friends with him. However, he constantly told us that "the Man" (white people) were no good, were devils, and could not be trusted. He made fun of our white friends and "preached" separatism of the races to the black kids. He ridiculed me when I told him my parents taught us that the skin color of a person did not matter, but a person was to be judged by the contents of his heart, and that there were good and bad in every race and nationality.

Even though he left for home earlier than anticipated, the "damage" was already done. Looking back, I understood how Adam and Eve must have felt when they bit into the fruit from the Tree of Knowledge that was forbidden by God. The scales of innocence and color blindness fell from my eyes. Before this point, I did not realize that I was any different from my white friends. I saw myself and my family, as well as my friends who were more like brothers and sisters, with new eyes and understanding. The "gang" eventually began to go our separate ways and was never as close as we had been before.

The exception would be the Clagg family, however. I spent many Friday nights playing Yahtzee with Juanita Clagg, who was remarried to Don Rutter, even after Debby married and moved away. Dad and I played cards with their family members, usually Juanita and Don, Sue, Sandy and Tony. We started the tradition of having family picnics with both families for many years. Debby and I were neighbors for a brief time when I bought a house next to hers on Walnut Street. That friendship has extended down to the third generation and continues today.

There have been many instances of racial prejudice, discrimination, and bigotry, too many to put in this book. Despite the sacrifices and commitment by various people and organizations and churches to bring about equality for all men, racial injustice continues today. People have been denied housing, even with couples where one is white and the other is black. If a black person moved into the "wrong" part of town, that person suffered racial slurs and had tomatoes and stones thrown at them or their children.

The West side of Lancaster has long been notorious for not accepting blacks. This is particularly true in a specific area on that side of town. Danny Smith, a 1959 Lancaster High School graduate, grew up in the family home located at the corners of South Columbus and Winding streets. He said he begged his dad, Emile Smith, to change the mailbox to Winding Street so that he could go to Thomas Ewing Junior High School with the other black kids. However, his dad refused to have it changed from 400 S. Columbus Street, so Danny had to go to General Sherman Junior High School on the west side. He was the only black student in the entire school. Although he had some difficult experiences, he said that he made a number of white friends who defended him when needed. He said the experience helped him to get along with people of all races, but at that time, he was glad to rejoin his black friends when they reached the high school level.

I recall one incident in 1977 that I experienced. I was home from college for the weekend and the family decided to have a Fat Cat is Pizza, from the establishment which was located on the west side. Normally Dad had it delivered, but this time he wanted me to pick it up. Since it was still light outside, I thought it would be okay. My youngest brother, Evan, wanted to ride with me, so we went to get it. When we left the pizzeria with our food, several large teens were standing close by and saw us. One said, "Look, there's a couple of niggers. What are they doing here?" I told Evan to hurry up and get in the car. Before I could pull off they surrounded my car and were trying to rock it, yelling racial slurs at us. I put my foot down hard on the gas, not really caring if I ran someone over or not, I knew I had to get out of there for our safety. It was a long time before I set foot on the west side again.

Another incident in the same west side neighborhood occurred almost twenty years later, in 1998--this time involving a single mother and her six children. The Black Interest Group is frequently called upon by other social service agencies for assistance, particularly when minorities are involved. The Lighthouse shelter for abused women and children is one such agency.

In October 1997, Yolanda Dyer moved to Lancaster with her children to escape domestic violence in Alabama. Little did she know that she would run into another form of abuse--racism and racial intimidation. Yolanda was moved into an apartment run by the shelter. It was nice, but it was on the west side, on Washington Avenue. She was called derogatory names before they got out of the car, yet the shelter's staff moved her into the apartment. During the few months the Dyers lived there, her door was jimmied, the bulb of her porch light was loosened and someone would knock on her door and then call her names and run when she looked out. Her children were called racial slurs and had things thrown at them as they walked to West Elementary School. Mary Good, a school social worker escorted them to and from school every day for fear of their safety.

On January 29, 1998 the situation came to a head. At 4 a.m., someone pounded on Yolanda's apartment door. She found a note stuck to the door calling them "niggers" and to go back home to Africa where they belonged. Yolanda called Mom and me. We went over and called the Lancaster police. The Black Interest Group appealed to the Lighthouse director several times to move them away from that neighborhood, but no one did anything.

After the above incident, Yolanda called her parents in Missouri and they arrived several days later to move her back home with them. On February 7, while they were moving out, the Black Interest Group and Peace Action of Lancaster organized a peaceful demonstration to denounce the blatant racism. About a dozen people, black and white, carried signs and marched up and down the street. Several prominent white residents included Priss Endo, Ed Robbins, Marilyn Walker and Rev. Bob Tussing with Grace Untied Church of Christ. They said they came to show the positive element of Lancaster. Several people in the neighborhood came by and told us they were not all prejudiced or racist. One teen joined the march and said that he was sorry that

Yolanda and her children were mistreated by a few people who lived on the street.

The *Lancaster Eagle-Gazette* and Columbus' Channel 4 News covered the incident. Yolanda told us she held no malice, that the police and mayor were good to her as well as very helpful. She insisted that she had no problems with Lancaster as a whole--just the area where she lived.

Another area where discrimination took place was the workplace. Qualified blacks have been denied jobs or promotions, or incurred overt racism on the job because of the darkness of their skin. Major places of employment, including the shoe factory, Anchor Hocking, the *Lancaster Eagle-Gazette*, and Diamond Power hired black janitors but would not allow them to work in other positions. During World War II, however, Alten Foundry on South Maple Street needed workers and gave black men jobs in the factory.

Black students within the school system have also had problems with students and teachers. Despite the growing population of black students, there still remain no black teachers, support staff, administrative staff or the Board of Education for which the black—with whom students can identify.

Within the community there have been countless incidents of prejudice and bigotry. Several black residents reported there were times when a white person would just stare with hate in their eyes at a black resident. I was on the receiving end of a store clerk who was very rude and threw money on the counter while handing money to the white customers. Such subtle forms of racism still happens more than people know.

On the positive side, for every person who spews or demonstrates prejudice, there is a large handful of whites who are supportive of the black community and do not condone racial prejudice. Ron Keaton, Joe Hoover, a former mayor of Bremen; Bill Daubenmire, former director of the Community Action Program of Fairfield County; Art Wallace, former mayor of Lancaster; Phil and Marilyn Walker, owners of Walker Shoe Store; and Rev. Robert Tussing, former pastor of Grace United Church, are just a few people of many who have been invaluable to the black community.

In 1995, I talked with several older white citizens who described for me how they perceived the black community through the years and if they thought there was any type of discrimination towards the local blacks. Virginia Hazelton, better known as "Ginny," a retired librarian at Lancaster High School and widow of the late Perrin "P.R." Hazelton, former publisher at *Lancaster Eagle-Gazette*, recalled only fond memories of local blacks, both past and present.

Ginny remembered Mary Thomas, a beautician, as being a gentle, soft-spoken lady. Ginny said when she was a young girl, she and her brothers played in the Thomas' backyard while waiting for their mother to get her hair done.

John and Oscar Hawkins were two outstanding football players while they were in high school, according to Ginny. She described Hazel Byrd as a very sweet lady. She said she always enjoyed riding with Byrd to Granville, Ohio to attend church services at an Episcopal church. Ginny also expressed high regards for Fred and Verna Preston. Fred worked at Fairfield School for Boys, and Verna worked as a volunteer for many years at the Community Action Head

Start program. Their son, Mike, as a young boy, often played at Ginny's house with her sons.

Ginny said she believed that whites, for the most part, supported the black community. She said when her son, Rick and her nephew, David Contosta were teachers at Lancaster high School in the 1970s, they taught classes in black history. However, there was not enough support at that time to continue the classes.

John "Jack" Kelley, a local attorney, also said he really had not witnessed any discrimination in Lancaster. He said the population of local blacks had always been small, and admitted he only had the opportunity to know a few. He spoke highly of Bill Stewart, the only black in the Lancaster High School Class of 1946. He said Bill was well-liked by everyone but was hesitant about attending the class senior prom. In order to help Bill feel comfortable, the class encouraged him to invite another black couple to attend the dance, and they paid for that couple's tickets. Bill invited his brother, Richard and two girls from Logan as their dates.

Bill went on to attend Ohio State University and Central State University, a black college in Xenia, Ohio. He earned his bachelor's and master's degrees in social work. He was a director of a halfway house for youth offenders in Rochester, New York until his death at the age of 51 in 1979.

Jack also recalled the presence of the KKK in Lancaster, but did not recall any acts of violence towards the black community.

Steps have been made through the years to bring about racial balance and equality. Two instances come from my personal experiences and observations. One is within the schools. During the 1960s and 70s, it was hard for the black students to be involved in extracurricular activities. A handful of black students played sports. In sports, my brothers, Kenny and Lawrence, as well as Steve Carlisle, Sam Nichols, and Ricky Stewart played football; Darryl and Juan Franklin ran track; and Juan and Rick Turner played basketball. It was harder for the girls. Although I had been a cheerleader at South School, I was laughed at when I showed up for try-outs in junior high. Although I did sing in the A Cappella Choir in high school, I could not be in Singing Gales, a select musical ensemble that performed in concerts at school and in the community.

Blacks were discouraged from being in the school plays. I cannot remember any blacks in the marching band. Much to the delight and support of majority of the student body, Kathy Fisher was nominated and elected as LHS Mirage Queen in 1970. Charlotte McKinley received the honors in 1971.

As the 1970s progressed in the 80s, it became easier for the blacks to be involved in whatever they wanted to do. My brother, AJ Saunders and Rodney Stewart broke school records in football during their high school years. Both were selected to play in the North-South All-Star High School Football game in Canton, Ohio. My younger brothers and sister were in school plays and musicals. Alan had a little trouble finding a partner who would dance with him, but he was in Singing Gales along with Victor Jones. Valeria had no problems being in Singing Gales, and no one thought about it when my youngest brother, Evan, made the group. In fact, Evan was a class officer, involved in sports, and voted "Mr. LHS."

In the 1990s and into 2000s, black students could participate in any activity they desired with little or no repercussions. A number of the black students played sports. No one could be any more talented and popular in basketball than the McKnight brothers--Phil, Chad, Chris, and Brett. Phil is playing professional basketball in Europe. Chad is finishing his college career in West Virginia. Chris graduated from Lancaster High School in 2006, and accepted a full college scholarship to Akron University. Chris was honored at the last game of the season when he surpassed the 1,000 point mark. On Feb. 28, 2006, during the Division I district tournament game, Chris surpassed Greg Clay, leading scorer record for the 1988-91, to became the top scorer in the history of Lancaster High School.

During his senior year, Brett was able to show off what he learned from his brothers. He was one of the leading scorers for the Lancaster Gales. He averaged 12 points and six rebounds per game, leading LHS to a 25-2 season. He was named as the fourth best wing/forward in the state of Ohio by PrepSpotlight. He received other honors which included selection as the Coaches Association's Division I Player of the Year, which is a very prestigious award. He was named the 2007 Associated Press All-Central District I Player of the Year. Brett was also selected as a Division I First-Team All-Ohio basketball player. He joined his three older brothers in receiving this honor. Brett will play with his brother Chris on a collegiate level when he attends Akron University in the fall of 2007.

The brothers' parents, Phil Sr. and Beth McKnight, have much to be proud of. From what I understand, Phil, Sr. played college basketball in Michigan. He continues to work as a unit manager at Southeastern Correctional Institution. He coaches peewee football during the fall and is pastor of a small church in Lancaster. Phil and Beth, of course, are their sons' biggest fans and continue to be a great source of encouragement and inspiration while keeping their feet firmly grounded.

Other blacks were cheerleaders, including Brandy Stoughton, granddaughter of Joe Carlisle, while others were student leaders, and were in school plays.

My daughter, Heather, a 2003 graduate, may have been the first black to play with the Swinging Gales, the noted musical group. She was also a four-year member of the Lancaster High School Band of Gold and was in the pep band, Symphonic Band and Concert Band. She appreciated the encouragement and support from her band teachers: Sandy McCoy, her first band teacher at Thomas Ewing Junior, High, Chris Bode at Stanbery Freshman School, and Chris Heidenreich at Lancaster High School.

Ashley Hughes, my niece and another 2003 graduate, carried on the Saunders tradition as a member of the Singing Gales. She also sang in the Concert, Symphonic and Chamber choirs. Her sister, Erin, who graduated in 2007, was also a member of Singing Gales during her junior year. Mrs. Lisa Springer was their choir director.

Kenya Hughes, the third daughter plays in the junior high band. But she has the distinction of being the only female on the Thomas Ewing football team. She played two years of peewee football with the champion Fairgrounds Cowboys and was selected as Offensive Lineman of the Year and Player of the Year. She was on the seventh and eighth grade football teams at Thomas Ewing Junior High School. Kenya said she wants to continue in football as long as she can. She also sings in the choir and hopes to be in Singing Gales when she reaches high school in the 2006-07 school year.

The second example of the black and white community reaching out to each other is the Masonic Temple, which is next door to Allen Chapel Church. It is well known that the Masonic Lodge does not permit blacks to be members of that lodge or of Rainbow for girls and Demolay for boys. In the mid-70s, my brother Alan was invited to visit Demolay and to become a member. He was excited and went to the Masonic Temple as instructed. However, he found out it was a cruel joke, and he was not permitted in. In 1980, when my sister Valeria was in Singing Gales, the group was invited to sing at a meeting at the Masonic Temple. When the group arrived and Valeria was spotted in the parking lot with the group, a member of the Masonic Lodge informed her she was not allowed inside. The group's director, Mr. Slyder, said if Valeria was not permitted in, they would not sing. She was allowed inside but had to leave immediately after they sang.

In the late 1990s and into 2000s, members reached out to the members of Allen Chapel, first by allowing us to park in their parking lot for church events if there were no activities at the Masonic Temple and then by offering to help with little projects around the church. In the spring of 2005, they agreed to allow several scenes of the Fairfield Heritage

Association's Black History Walk to take place inside their building. To me, and others, this was a momentous occasion. I have to admit that I was very nervous when I first stepped inside the door into the hallway, and it took awhile to feel comfortable going in and out, as we carried in the scenery and props. Several people said they could not bring themselves to go in. I would be very surprised if the Masonic Lodge would open their doors to black members; however, I see and applaud the small changes as they slowly reached out to their black neighbors.

It is the hope of the Black Interest Group that people in Lancaster and Fairfield County will continue to respond to the challenges put forth by Dr. King decades ago, challenges that have yet fully to come to fruition, the challenge that all citizens, both black and white, must come together and ask what can we do and do it. The late Rev. Chuck Fisher once said, "We've come a long way in regard to black prejudice, but we still have a long way to go. It still exists. It will exist until we understand each other, recognize our differences, and accept our differences and our sameness." Only when this is done will all barriers--physical, mental, social, and economical--be brought down and destroyed forever.

Chapter 6

Helping to Fight the Good Fight

In the closing years of the turbulent 1960s, the black students continued to experience problems with both students and teachers. Several teachers, including David Contasta and William Schorr met on several occasions with my Mom to discuss these problems and possible solutions. About the same time, the Catholic community had a social function and residents of the Fairfield School for Boys provided musical entertainment. A number of black citizens accepted an invitation to attend the function. Afterwards, a discussion between the boys from FSB and the local blacks took place about the forms of discrimination they have experienced. The Catholic priest and nun, Father Mario and Sister Caroline seemed to be surprised and admitted they were not aware that these problems occurred in Lancaster. As a result, they arranged to have a panel discussion that was open to the public. The panel consisted of four Catholic teens and four black teens: my brother Kenny and I, Sam Nichols, Jr. and Juan Franklin.

The open and honest discussion that took place brought new enlightenment to the black and white communities of Lancaster. For months afterwards, the civic and business leaders expressed concern about the plight of the local black citizens and talked about their desire to help bring about meaningful changes. They met several times with several blacks, including Ken and Alice Saunders, Dolores Carlisle and Joan Carlisle. From this, the Lancaster Chapter of the NAACP, or National Association for the Advancement of Colored People, was formed in 1969.

A meeting was held to elect officers for the newly formed chapter. A slate of officers was set to be presented; however, a group of blacks that had not previously been involved with any of the previous discussions or planning stepped in and completely took over. No one on the original slate of officers was voted to hold any type of office.

The first president was Grant Grogans, with Stanley "Buddy" Carlisle as vice-president. Sister Caroline Humphrey actively supported the NAACP as a member, as did Father Mario until his transfer to another diocese. However, I was told that a number of the white people who were in on the planning withdrew their support.

In recognition of the formation of the local NAACP chapter, then Lancaster Mayor William E. Burt issued a proclamation declaring Saturday, November 8, 1969, as NAACP Day in Lancaster. That same evening, the charter-commissioning banquet was held at Shaw's Steak House. Guest speaker for the event was William H. Williams, president of the Columbus chapter of the NAACP. It was reported that 140 guests from all over Ohio attended. Grant Grogans was presented with the charter from second State Vice-President Warren Pate of Columbus. Standing with Grogans to receive the charter were Stanley Carlisle, vice president of the Lancaster NAACP; Rev. James Parker, pastor of Grace Baptist Church; Father Diamond of St. Mark's Catholic Church; and Mrs. Helen Carlisle, mistress of ceremonies for the banquet and member of the Lancaster NAACP.

During the early years of the chapter, the members were very active and succeeded in opening doors of communication, which resulted in some of the problems being corrected. However, it did not succeed in unifying the black community.

One of the highlights for blacks during this time was the Black Studies Series held at the Ohio University-Lancaster campus. Dr. Ron Ziska taught the series. The planning for the classes came about from the discussions with my mother, Alice Saunders, Dr. Ziska, Mr. Contasta and Mr. Schorr before the NAACP chapter was formed. The classes were well received and attended by both black and white citizens.

The local chapter held its annual Freedom fund banquet and had a variety of interesting speakers. The banquet also served as a way to raise money and membership. Monthly meetings were held and sometimes a guest speaker was on hand. One speaker was H.N. Larnell Leggins, an officer from the U.S. Federal Defense Contracts Compliance Office in Cleveland. He was also a math professor at Cuyahoga College. He spoke at the November 26, 1969 event and emphasized the importance of higher education and training to be prepared for jobs and careers.

In May 1970, the local NAACP sponsored a commemorative program to celebrate the historical decision of the U.S. Supreme Court is decision on May 17, 1954 that ruled that segregation in public schools was illegal. This program was held at Stanbery Junior High School. The guest speaker was Attorney William J. Davis, a well-known Civil Rights lawyer. His speech emphasized the importance of receiving a good education. He also stressed the importance of being a registered voter and going out to vote on election days.

In addition to the Black Studies classes, the local NAACP also sponsored other training classes. One such class was a training program held in cooperation with Anchor Hocking Corporation., Ohio Bureau of Employment Compensation, and the Lancaster City School System. Alice Saunders was the coordinator of the program.

The program included office work and related subjects, and production machine operations.

Several years after the formation of the Lancaster NAACP chapter, a youth chapter was started. Grant Grogans appointed David Moxley as interim chairman. However, it only lasted for about two or three years.

The local NAACP chapter saw a rise in membership in the early years of its existence and eventually a decline in the late 70s and early '80s. People in leadership positions paid little attention to the problems of the majority of the members and did not cooperate with many of the white community leaders who were working to solve any racial issues. A number of blacks became frustrated and dropped their membership after being denied assistance and because a small group of people who were in the leadership positions reduced the chapter to a private social club.

Several people served as president of the local NAACP with the hope of keeping the chapter active. These people were Stanley "Buddy" Carlisle, Tony Preston and Daisy Flowers. Daisy Flowers worked hard to remove the rift between the two groups of blacks and to restore the chapter to what it once was. Despite her efforts, she was not successful, and the chapter disbanded in 1982

The late 1970s and 80s witnessed a blending in the Lancaster community to the place where few blacks socialized together. Allen Chapel Church was no longer the major provider of the spiritual, social, and educational needs of the black community. With the social changes, blacks were no longer prohibited nor discouraged from associating with whites and could go just about anywhere they wanted. New families were beginning to move into Lancaster. Because of the very small percentage of blacks who lived in the city, some of the new families said they were not aware of other blacks who live here. I remember several instances where Mom and I met several different black people, and we were shocked that they had lived here for several years and had not met any other blacks. They all said they were beginning to think they were the only minority people in town.

During this time period, Mom was asked to sit on the YWCA Board of Directors. She heard friends and other people she met talk about discrimination problems they experienced in the workplace. Mom talked with Alice

Morrow, then director of the YWCA, and other board members about these problems. The two Alices decided after several months, why not start a force that worked personally with those who had problems as they arose. Several weeks later, they decided on this advocacy group, later named the Black Interest Group of Lancaster. Mom talked with me and Dad, and decided that the group could serve two purposes. There is little recorded information on black residents of Lancaster and Fairfield County. With Dad being one of the older native residents if Lancaster and with my having always had a special interest in research and recording history, we agreed. We became co-founders of the Black Interest Group.

About the same time, a Soul Picnic was held at Rising Park, and we invited old and new residents. We also invited some of the white people who had been active in the NAACP and were always willing to assist the black community. The picnic was well attended, and everyone had so much fun that the attendees voted to make it an annual event.

The next year, the second annual Soul Picnic was held at Rising Park as a way to bring old and new black residents together. Everyone enjoyed the fellowship although not many were in attendance. A meeting was held, and those in attendance discussed various problems the blacks have experienced. They agreed there was a need to have some type of organization for blacks for socialization, support, and problem solving. After the picnic, I attended several meetings with Kenneth and Alice Saunders, Eugene Booker, Mary Nichols, Sam Nichols, Jr., Ruby Fisher, Mary Keels, and Lawrence Saunders in attendance. It was during these meetings that the name of the group was selected, and the group's statement of purpose was written.

On September 2, 1982, Kenneth Mace, who was mayor of Lancaster at that time, wrote a letter recognizing the formation of this new organization, which was officially named the Black Interest Group (BIG) of Lancaster. In the early years of the organization, a 12-member volunteer executive board was in place.

The original officers of the Black Interest Group were as follows:

Alice Saunders, president

Eugene Booker, vice president

Hollie Saunders, co-founder and public relations

Shirley Jones, secretary

Kenneth Saunders, Sr., co-founder and treasurer

Lawrence Saunders, advisory and legal consultant

The committees included:

Activity and program: Mary Keels

Edna Fay Saunders

Eugene Booker

Ruby Fisher

Black Heritage: Hollie Saunders

Dolores Carlisle

Edna Fay Saunders

Kenneth Saunders, Sr.

Additional members were:

Sam Nichols, Jr.

Song Nicolia

Gladys Keels

Verna Preston

Members-at-large were:

Mary Nichols

Alice Morrow

Attorney Ed Beery

Mayor Kenneth Mace

The following months were busy with meetings to write the goals, purpose, and by-laws for the group.

The following year, 1983, seemed to be the year of the Black Heritage Movement in Lancaster. While February was set aside on a nationwide basis, Black History Month was observed by the Fairfield County Public Library by having a display of art, sculpture and woodworking projects by local black artists. Kenneth Saunders, Jr., a 1970 LHS graduate contributed several paintings and sculptures. As a multi-media artist he works with computer graphics, design, graphic illustrations, painting, and photography. James Saunders, a 1959 graduate, was well known for his paintings and sculptures. He had two paintings in the art show. Dolores Carlisle, another gifted painter and a 1955 graduate, contributed two paintings. The other contributing artists for that exhibit were the Jones brothers, James, Larry, and Jonathon. James, a 1978 graduate, produced a series of driftwood carvings done with a pocketknife and several pencil sketches. Larry, a 1979 graduate, contributed a cannon made from brass and a woodcarving. Jonathon, a 1982 graduate, displayed a chess table and hand-tooled chessmen that took him three years to make.

In 1983, Rev. Chuck Fisher, a regular columnist for the *Lancaster Eagle-Gazette*, and a white minister who was considered to be close friends to many people in the black community, wrote stirring articles about his experiences and memories of local black citizens. The managing editor of the *Lancaster Eagle-Gazette* asked me to write a series of articles about the local black heritage.

That same year, the Black Interest Group also decided to host a banquet to celebrate their accomplishments. Mary Ann Theller and Barbara Lynch were instrumental in the planning and the program of the first banquet. Members also thought that it would be fitting to recognize those individuals who made a significant contribution to the black community. This recognition came in the form of the Heartline to the Community Award. The first award was given to Mary Burnham, who made sure the black youth of the 40s and 50s were able to have parties and gatherings at the YM-YWCA. The organization also voted to name the award in her honor to exemplify her heartfelt concern and outreach to the black community.

Each year at the banquet, a speaker or guest artist or entertainer is featured. Over the years, we have had a variety of programs and guest speakers or artists, including the following:

1983 - "Spotlighting Local Black Talent" at the Knights of Columbus Hall. Mary Ann Theller on piano with singing by Hollie, Alan, Valeria, and Evan Saunders, Linda Carlisle, Eugene Booker and Eugene Turner.

1984 - "Memories" at Knights of Columbus Hall. Joan Carlisle directed a style show and music from four different eras - 1900-30; 1931-50, 1951-70; and 1971-83

1985 - "Back to Our Roots" at the Fairfield County District Library Main Branch. African students from Ohio University provided African music and dance.

1986 - "Footprints of the Past" at Knights of Columbus Hall. Rev. Chuck Fisher talked about his memories and relationship with Lancaster's black community.

1987 - "Dance and Fellowship" at the Holiday Inn. Music was provided by the Slappy Family from Columbus.

1988 - "We've Come This Far" at the Holiday Inn. Speaker was Dr. Vettle Rose, Professor of Afro-American studies at Ohio University, Athens.

1989 - "Keeping the Dream Alive" at Holiday Inn. Speaker was Dana Tyler, news anchor at WBNS Channel 10 News, Columbus.

1990 - "Looking Towards the Future" at Holiday Inn. Earl Edwards of Cleveland talked about what the black community had to do to stay competitive in the future. His twin sister, professional musician, Denise Edwards, also of Cleveland, danced and sang.

1991 - "Sing a Song of Praise, Tears, and Joy" at Holiday Inn. Professional entertainer, Ethel Caffee-Austin performed and had interactive musical activities with the audience.

1992 - "We've Come This Far by Faith" at Holiday Inn. Music provided by the Saunders Family Singers.

1993 - "Moving On Up" at the Elks Lodge. A Slide Show presentation of past banquets as presented and narrated by Hollie Saunders. Denise Edwards provided musical program.

1994 - "Striving For the Dream" at Holiday Inn. Guest speaker was Dr. Barbara Ross-Lee, dean of the Ohio University School of Osteopathic Medicine. Dr. Ross Lee is also the sister of legendary Motown singer, Diana Ross. In addition to the medical school, Dr. Ross-Lee talked about what it was like growing up with Diana and being around other Motown legends, including Stevie Wonder, Smokey Robinson, and Marvin Gaye.

1995 - "Harmony" at Holiday Inn. Louise Cassandra and the Fred Astaire Dancers presented the program.

1996 - "Back to Our Roots." at Best Western. Dr. Marc Miller, local psychologist and writer, explorer and hunter of exotic animas with Jack Hanna, director of the Columbus Zoo, talked about his trip to Africa.

1997 - "Come to the BIG Cabaret" at the FOP Lodge. African dancers and drummers were part of the program.

1998 - Judge Janet Jackson of Columbus was guest speaker; The Saunders Family presented a musical history of singing together.

1999 - "Working Together For the Youth" at Best Western. Speakers who talked about the plight of today's youth and how to guide them in positive manner included Kean McGill, director of the Youth Boxing League, Jerry Paige, professional boxer, and Judge Janet Jackson of Columbus.

2000 - "Swinging into the New Millennium" at Best Western. Pianist and singer Joyce Meade performed.

2001 - "An Evening with Old Friends" at Best Western. Local recording folk singers Mike Wood, Anne Kiphen, and Nick Weiland provided musical program.

2002 - "We've Come This Far by Faith" at First United Methodist Church. Music was provided by professional singer, Beverly Carroll of Columbus, accompanied on piano by Roxanne Reid, also of Columbus. The Lancaster Community Band under the direction of Judy Rehrer presented pre-dinner music. Heather Saunders, LHS junior and member of the LHS Marching Band of Gold and Swinging Gales sat in with the band and played the baritone saxophone. Ashley Hughes, LHS junior and member of the Swinging Gales, sang several big band era songs.

As a surprise, Alice Saunders, President of the Black Interest Group was recognized for her dedication and work for the organization. Throughout the evening, emceed by Ron Keaton, she received letters, commendations, and plaques from the Fairfield County Community Action Board of Trustees; the Fairfield County Commissioners, Lancaster Mayor Art Wallace, the Ohio House of Representatives signed by State Representative Tim Schaffer and State senator Larry Householder; Lancaster City council; and The United States Congress signed by Congressman Dave Hobson.

All of the above were either present or sent a representative. Also attending was former Congressman Clarence Miller.

2003- "Down Home Fun with Ellen" at Best Western. Professional folk life artist Ellen Ford of Lancaster talked about the history of folk music and the different instruments associated with folk music, in particular Appalachian folk music. The audience's favorite was the hammer dulcimer. Ellen also got the audience involved by playing early American games.

2004 - "The History of Black Music" at Best western. Professional musician and recording artist Arnett Howard of Columbus talked about the evolution of jazz and black music from the 1800s until today. He also played the trumpet and sang. Pre-dinner music was provided by Ellen Ford on the hammer dulcimer.

2005 - "Striving For Excellence" at Best Western. Pre-dinner music was provided by Ellen Ford on hammer dulcimer. Guest speaker was Dr. Roderick McDavis, incoming president of Ohio University.

2006 - "A Walk Through Time." Guest speaker was Deward Watts, associated with the Fairfield Heritage Association, talked about his research on black history and the coming together of the Black History Walk presented by the Black Interest Group and the Fairfield Historical Association in April of 2005. Two scenes from this program were re-enacted. The first scene involved Emmanuel Carpenter portrayed by Joe Griffith) and Scipio Smith, portrayed by Anthony Saunders. They discussed the possibility of Carpenter donated land to the black community for school and church purposes. Scipio Smith became the first minister of the black church. The second scene involved Rube Moss, portrayed by Bruce Johnson and Bertha Moss, portrayed by Toni Saunders. Rube was a successful business owner and his wife, Bertha was a successful hairdresser.

2007 – "Our Dream is Still Alive" at Lancaster Inn. Rev. Joel King of Gahanna, first cousin to Martin Luther King Jr. was the guest speaker for the group's 25th anniversary. Rev. King has been a member of the Ohio Dr. Martin Luther King Jr. Holiday Commission since 1985. In 2000, Gov. Bob Taft appointed him to represent Ohio on the Dr. Martin Luther King, Jr. National Holiday Advisory Committee. Rev. King is currently chaplain for the Gahanna Police Department. Special music was provided by Mary Ann Theller and a group of her young music students known as the Fairfield County Strings and Keyboard.

As much fun as the banquets are and the fact that people always look forward to them, they are not the main focus of the Black Interest Group. The Black Interest Group is a non-profit organization that acts as a vehicle to inform people that the black community is a viable part of Lancaster. The black community wanted their problems to be recognized, for civic and business communities to understand these problems, and to work together so that steps could be taken towards solutions of these problems.

The Black Interest Group believes that people can solve many problems if the parties involved are able to sit down and talk. The organization's role is more as a mediator between people having problems. The main intent of Black Interest Group is to strive to keep the dream of Martin Luther King Jr., alive, the dream that all men of all races will live and work together in understanding, peace, and harmony. Keeping this in mind, the organization has five objectives:

- *to act as a support system and advocate for all people if problems arise;*

- *to act as a referral system to assist in educational, occupational, legal, and civic matters for all people;*

- to encourage black citizens to be a part of Lancaster by creating a better understanding and appreciation of concerns or problems of blacks and other minorities;

- to provide information to black citizens regarding political and civic issues of Lancaster and Fairfield County;

- and to preserve the heritage of the black citizens by researching and recording their past and present history.

Members of the Black Interest Group stresses there is no race, religion, sex or age limitations for those whom they may assist. The Black Interest Group is registered with the State of Ohio and listed with Lancaster's Information and Crisis Referral Source. Many other social service organizations, businesses, and individuals have called upon the organization to assist them in various situations.

Mom has always been the backbone of the Black Interest Group and a respected member of the community. Born in Hocking County, Alice was raised in a predominantly white farming community. She and her brothers were the only black people at the small country school in Carbon Hill. She always said she was no specific race, just "Alice." Her maternal grandmother was a blond Scotch-Irish woman and her grandfather was half-black, half-Creek Indian (his mother was said to have been a runaway slave who was taken in by the Creek Indians and eventually married one of the Indians.) Her mother looked Indian, and her father was a light-skinned biracial man, told by other family members to have been half French-Canadian and half Cherokee Indian.

Because of the make-up of the community, and of her family background, it was not until her 16th birthday in the 1930s, that Alice experienced any racial issues. She often tells us about how she went to Hamilton, Ohio with her sister, Mabel, to visit relatives. She went to the movies with a cousin and sat in front of the theatre. During the movie, an usher came and told her they could not sit in front, and they had to either move or leave. Alice became angry and left. She asked her cousins why blacks accepted the rule that they had to sit in the back of the theatre. She was ready to march in protest. This incident always stuck with Mom and spurred her to fight the injustice dealt to her and to others. At 80 years of age, she is still ready to lead a march.

As I have stated earlier, Mom has been active in the community since the late 1960s. She has been on the board of directors for several organizations including the YW-YMCA, League of Women Voters, Human Resource Council, and Meals on Wheels. She was also very active with the Community Action Board of Directors in its early years. She was instrumental in bringing to Lancaster the food stamp program and the Head Start Program. Joe Hoover, president of the Community Action board recognized Mom's service to the board of directors, which started in July of 1984. Hoover said that even at her first board meeting, Mom began dialogue with the staff and board members that eventually resulted in the placement of a playground at Hunter's Trace apartment complex, a community for low-income residents. Later, as chair of the Human Rights

Committee, Mom was involved in the development of the agency's Affirmative Action plan. Joe said that Mom also served on the Executive Committee and was very helpful in the development of the agency as it grew in size and scope of services.

In the late 1960s and early 1970s, Mom and Dad were both involved with the Lancaster Montessori School, while Dad was one of the first members of the Lancaster Regional Planning Commission. In 1999, Mom was recognized as a finalist for the Columbus Dispatch Community Service Award. Mom currently serves as a member of the Southeastern Correctional Institution Community Advisory Board.

Alice Morrow, former director of the local YMCA, who now lives in Delaware, Ohio, credits Mom and the Black Interest Group with making the white community aware of the problems within the black community, and applauded her work to bring about positive changes. She said it was the compassion, understanding, and availability of Mom that "endless problems have been quietly met." These same qualities, according to Alice, have helped Mom and the Black Interest Group to establish cooperation between blacks and Fairfield County Sheriff's Office, the Lancaster Police Department, the Lancaster City Schools, churches and various local agencies. Morrow said, "It is in this spirit of cooperation that brings everyone together in the community."

When Alice Morrow first arrived in Lancaster in 1970, she said she noticed that the black community took care of their own problems and did not seem to reach out to the white community. She also said that she has not witnessed any type of overt discrimination against local black residents. However, she gradually became aware of subtle discrimination in the areas of employment, housing and within the school system. She attributed a lack of suitable jobs for blacks, in addition to the discrimination as reasons why many blacks do not work or live in Lancaster.

Different people I have talked with, both black and white, said they would like to see more blacks working on the professional level and in city and county departments, such as the police and fire departments, as well as within the city and county schools. In saying this, an interesting issue was raised - are there no blacks in these capacities because of racial discrimination or because there are no local blacks qualified for those positions. If blacks from surrounding areas worked in Lancaster but did not move here, is it prejudice or is it because of their preference to live where they could be around more blacks than live here. Also, if there are no blacks who attend community functions or hold memberships in local clubs and organizations, is it because blacks are not welcomed or is it because blacks do not express an interest in participating in these activities? Are the black citizens willing to extend themselves if the white citizens are just as willing?

I like what Jeannie Azbell once said: "We all have problems, no matter what color we happen to be. We need to learn to live together and work together as one people and one community to make Lancaster the best it can be for everyone who chooses to live and work here."

This is a good way to sum up what the Black Interest Group's goal is for all people in Lancaster. The Black Interest Group, along with the Lancaster Area Peacemakers, Grace

United Brethren Church and Maple Street United Methodist Church began to put together an annual celebration and memorial service on the state and federal recognized holiday, Dr. Martin Luther King, Jr. Day. The first event was held in January 1987 and was held at Maple Street United Methodist Church under the pastoral guidance of Rev. Larry Swaisgood. The church continued to host the event for many years. Several church and community leaders encouraged the group to include a peaceful march from the downtown bandstand to the church. In 1990, the march took place. About 75 people gathered at the bandstand for prayer and then the participants, carrying signs, a banner, and the American flag, received a police escort to the church. The number of attendees increased at the church. Then-mayor Don Maddux gave a short presentation prior to reading a proclamation designating that day as Martin Luther King, Jr. Day in Lancaster. In his presentation, Maddux stressed the importance of continuing to "resolve and reflect on Dr. King's ideals and dreams."

The guest speaker was Daisy Flowers, who had been president of the Lancaster and Columbus chapters of the NAACP, as well as a member of the Columbus Urban League, Ohio Historical Board of Trustees, and the Afro-American National Council of History and Culture.

Special guest speakers and entertainers have been featured at the King's Day services. Some of them included Rev. Robert Graetz, a white Lutheran minister who worked closely with Dr. King, and, as a result, had his home fire bombed; Betty Mitchell, the first black female warden at Southeastern Correctional Institution; and the Paul Laurence Dunbar Choir from Columbus.

The white community, even moreso than the black community, has embraced the celebration each year. The only incident came about the second year of the march. We received anonymous phone calls a few weeks before the march and service in which the person threatened to disrupt the march and service in some way. He said something to the effect that the "niggers here are never satisfied; you let them do one thing, and they have to do more." Concerned for the safety of the participants, there was a short discussion to cancel. However, the majority of the group said, no, because then the violence would win over peaceful demonstration and that King never backed down. Little did that person know that it was the white people who wanted to march in keeping of what King and other freedom fighters did during the Civil Rights Movement.

On the day of the service, the Lancaster Police Department had several cruisers escort the march with plain clothed officers placed along the parade route and outside the church. The march and service went with no problems.

Several years ago, Maple Street United Methodist Church, under the pastorate of Rev. Don Meadows, withdrew their support and abruptly withdrew their offer to host the event, just a month before the holiday. Mary Good was kind enough to ask her church, St. Bernadette Catholic Church to hold it there. Not only did Father Justin Reis agree, but the women of the church also catered a lunch for the participants after the service to allow people to eat and fellowship with each other.

In 2003, the venue changed to Grace United Brethren Church with Mary remaining as one of the driving forces behind the celebratory service. However, just days before the service, Mary was struck and killed by a car as she exited a beauty salon on Columbus Street, and was on her way to have lunch with co-workers at Annie's on Main Street. That service was dedicated to Mary and her tireless efforts to help people of all ages and skin color.

For the past three years, the First Presbyterian Church has given their support and the use of their church for the services. The celebration has been more than remembering King but as a way to remember that we as a human race must continue to come together and fight the nonsense of racism. Organizers have always tried to get people to remember that because it is more than a day to get off work or out of school. It is a day to honor King and the memory of other civil rights workers by helping others remember the horrors inflicted by "Jim Crow" and the separatist mentality that try to keep a race of people down for having a different skin color.

In 2006, the celebration centered around Rosa Parks, whose brave decision not to give up her seat on the bus in Montgomery, Alabama, sparked the beginning of the Great Civil Rights Movement and catapulted Dr. Martin Luther King, Jr. into the forefront of the Movement. The Lancaster Transit Authority provided a bus and participants rode the bus through the downtown area as they sang the Civil Rights anthem, "We Shall Overcome".

It was a sad day in January 2006 when Coretta Scott King, the widow of Dr. Martin Luther King, Jr. died after a battle with ovarian cancer. Coretta picked up her husband's mantle and carried out the work he began up until the time of her death. She was honored with a moment of silence at the Black Interest Group's annual banquet.

Since the beginning of the Black Interest Group, members have been involved on various community committees for the betterment of the city as a whole. We have talked with the police to facilitate better relations between police officers and the black community and to encourage the hiring of black officers. There have been several qualified black candidates who applied for a position on the local police department but were not hired. Several black officers tried to transfer from Columbus to Lancaster but were not successful. To me, it is almost unbelievable that Lancaster's only black police officer was on the force over a century ago.

For several years, I was a guest speaker at the local Sheriff's Training Academy taught by Lt. Gary Kennedy. I talked about discrimination and how to better understand and deal with blacks.

We have also talked with administrators of the local school system about problems involving any student who asked for assistance, including when there was a concern about gangs in the school. Because of Mom's insistence that there was a problem with gangs, a committee was formed. As a result, the problem was uncovered and dealt with. Rev. Aaron Wheeler of Columbus, a minister who has dealt extensively with gangs, conducted workshops, and has written a book, spoke to the committee. He also conducted a workshop about how to recognize gang activity within the schools and the community.

In 1983, my brother, Lawrence, represented the Black Interest Group to advocate for a better disaster plan and warning system in Lancaster. Because of his personal experience with a natural disaster, he said he was not satisfied with the lack of a warning system. At that time, if there were a pending disaster, the police turned on their sirens, traveled through the city, and warned people to take appropriate steps.

Lawrence, and our oldest brother, Kenny were attending college at Central State University at Wilberforce in 1974 when one of the worst tornadoes on record devastated Xenia and the areas surrounding it. Four students were killed on the campus, and more than 40 people died in Xenia.

I remember that was one of the longest nights I had ever experienced. I was home from Ohio University on spring break. My parents and I heard on the news about the tornado and immediately began to worry and pray for Kenny and Lawrence. We were unable to get in touch with them because all power and lines were out. We contacted the Red Cross who were as helpful as they could be at that time. All we could do was pray they were safe and not injured and that they would be able to call us. The next morning they called us and reassured us they were not hurt and asked for us to drive down and pick them up. As we neared what was left of Xenia and the college campus, it was hard to believe what we were seeing.

Lawrence told us that a Dayton radio station announced that a tornado was headed toward Xenia. Shortly after that, the electricity went out, and within five minutes or less, he and other students could see the tornado going towards the campus. He said it was so large it looked more like a dust storm than a funnel cloud, and many people were fascinated by it and had to be pulled to safety. He said they could see a lot of Xenia in the sky. Because there were no organized places to go for shelter, everyone ran into buildings and tried to get the basements. He said it was fortunate that most of the students and faculty were already in the buildings for classes. If it had hit five minutes later, classes would have been over and more people would have been outside heading for home, which would have probably resulted in more deaths.

The tornado went directly for the building that Lawrence and Kenny were in. He said they heard a crumbling crashing noise, and they all thought the building would cave in on them. A rush of wind shook the building. Lawrence said he felt like the wind picked him up off the floor. Kenny said he had to push a girl to safety because she could not stop looking at it. He did not get his leg all the way through the door and said the wind sucked his shoe off his foot, but he was not injured.

Just as quickly as the winds came, they were suddenly left in complete silence.

My brothers said they ran outside and could immediately see the destruction. Lawrence said the top floor of the building they were in had been blown away and the second floor suffered severe damage. Other parts of the campus sustained heavy damages. Many people thought the school would be forced to close; however, it was rebuilt with the generous donations by alums and other concerned people, including the famous actor/entertainer, Dr. Bill Cosby. The building that houses the School of Communications is named in his honor.

Lancaster's lack of an adequate warning system concerned Lawrence, especially if a tornado hit at night when people were sleeping. He said he wanted to make sure Lancaster had some protection from what happened in Xenia. It was not until 1993 that a citywide siren warning system was installed in case of a tornado or other impending disaster.

Chapter 7

Names and Faces that Broke Through the Barrier

The 1940s and 50s saw the hard work, determination and sacrifices of Lancaster's local black residents. The 1960s was a decade of awakening, of awareness of the right for equal opportunity in all areas for all humanity. As a result, the black youth of the 1970s and 80s were among the first not only to contribute their skills and knowledge to the community with little problems but also to excel in their endeavors. Many of these young people were noted and recognized by the residents of Lancaster for their accomplishments in different areas--in the military, social services, music and in sports. Most of the people mentioned in this chapter are the ones who broke through the color barrier to pave a path for those in the 1990s and 2000s to walk proudly without stumbling as often because of their race.

When Uncle Sam called forth those men to fight in World War II, The Korean War and the Vietnam War, many blacks responded to the call. I thought it would be appropriate to pay homage to those who served their country, even at time when they were treated as less than equals by their fellow citizens. Thankfully all who served returned home safely.

World War II and the Korean War created the most black veterans from Lancaster. The most noted person was Captain Charles Hawkins, who made the military his career. He was highly decorated throughout his career. During World War II, Hawkins was a military police officer with the 558th M.P. Company. On January 14, 1969, President Lyndon B. Johnson awarded Hawkins with the Meritorious Service Medal. He was also recognized for Outstanding Achievement for Mission in Physical Security for Critical Special Ammunition Storage. Hawkins retired in 1978.

Other black veterans from those eras are as follows: Oscar Hawkins, Jr., Albert Hawkins, Bill Anderson, Albert Jones, John Wesley Moss, Floyd Saunders, Lewis Wolfe, "Skinny" Martin, Bill McKinley, Kenneth "Sock" Saunders, Sr.; Charles "Brother" Hunster. Charles Allen, Stanley Turner, Walter Moxley, Ralph Sliuce, Henry Preston, Stanley "Buddy" Carlisle, Sam Nichols, Sr., Stanley H. Carlisle and Joe Carlisle, Charles Carlisle, Francis Ely, Pearl Hawkins, and Bill Stewart.

Several servicemen survived the controversial Vietnam War. They are Kenneth Saunders, Jr., Franklin Keels, Jr., Victor Carlisle, and Sam Nichols, Jr.

Sam Nichols, Jr. entered the Army upon graduation from Lancaster High School in 1972. He was reportedly in the Demilitarized War Zone with the 2nd Infantry Division. In 1980, he was discharged with the rank of sergeant.

Victor Carlisle reportedly served two tours of duty in Vietnam while in the Navy.

Kenneth Saunders, Jr. enlisted in the Marine Corps after his graduation in from LHS in 1970. He was the first trainee to open the Marine Corps School of Construction Drafting, One of Kenneth's major contributions was the designing of a park in Barbers Point Naval Air Station, Hawaii. He also saw combat in Vietnam. Kenneth was discharged in 1974. He then attended Central State University in Xenia, where he studied architectural design. He became a freelance artist and designer in computer graphics. He was selected to design and paint the "Freedom Wall" that is seen in the movie "Brubaker." He now lives near San Francisco with his wife, Mary Ann.

Franklin Keels, Jr. is one of the most highly decorated black soldiers from Lancaster. Frank graduated from LHS in 1968 and immediately entered the military. He graduated from the U.S. Army Military Police School at Fort Gordon, Georgia. He served two terms in Vietnam with the American Infantry Division, 23rd Military Police Company. He reportedly received numerous awards and Army Commendation Medals.

After discharge from the Army, Keels became a member of the Ohio Air National Guard at Rickenbacker Air Force Base. He was a T/Sgt. with the 121st Security Police FLT as a flight chief. In 1980, Frank was named the Outstanding Guardsman for the 121st TFW. He also was awarded various Air Force Medals and honors. He now lives in Colorado with his wife, Mary.

Bruce Carlisle, Randy Prichett, and Kevin Saunders served in the military during the years following the Vietnam War. Bruce Carlisle, a 1972 Lancaster High School graduate, served in the U.S. Navy from 1973 to 1977. He was honored with many distinctions and awards during his stint in the Navy. He attended the Hospital Corps School N.T.C. in Great Lakes, Illinois, and graduated in the top ten percent of his class. He also received two Meritorious Masts for outstanding service with the U.S. Marine Corps and was selected as Sailor of the Month and Sailor of the Quarter while with the 1st Medical Battalion, 1st FSSG. After his discharge, Bruce attended West Virginia Wesleyan College and graduated in 1982 with a bachelor's degree in biology with a minor in chemistry.

Like Bruce Carlisle, Randy Pritchett is a 1972 Lancaster High School graduate, where he was an outstanding football and track star. He was also junior class president. Randy is reportedly the first black from Lancaster to be appointed to, attend, and graduate from the U.S. Naval Academy. While at the Naval Academy, Randy lettered from 1974 through 1976 both in indoor and outdoor track. He was co-captain of the Midshipman runners his senior year. Randy graduated in 1976 with a major in Economics. As a naval flight officer, he earned his wings in 1978 while stationed in Pensacola, Florida. He was a captain in the Marine Air Corps and was stationed at Cherry Point, North Carolina, where he pursued a master's degree in systems analysis.

Kevin Saunders, a 1979 LHS graduate trained at Lackland Air Force Base in San Antonio, Texas after his induction in the Air National Guards in November of 1979. He attended the Security Police Combat School while at

Lackland AFB and completed emergency service training, which is equivalent to the civilian police's SWAT team. Kevin served as a security police officer at Rickenbacker Air Force Base near Columbus while in the Air Guards. After several years he entered the Air Force fulltime. He was stationed at Lackland AFB where he was a drill instructor and a classroom instructor. He most recently was stationed at Eldornorf Air Force Base in Anchorage, Alaska, where he was head of security. He is now reassigned to Edwards Air Force Base in California and has the rank of Master Sergeant. Kevin also fought in Desert Storm and the current war on terrorism in the Middle East. He was assigned to Edwards Air Force Base with his wife, Frances and three children and retired last month. He will be teaching ROTC at a high school outside of Charlotte.

In the civilian world, there were a number of blacks who made significant strides and personal success, therefore, beating the odds of being held back because of their race. These people refused to be pigeon-holed and worked in their chosen professions regardless of the challenges faced with being sometimes the only black person in a sea of white people.

Francis "Sis" McKinley was the first black to work at the Lancaster hospital. She worked there as a nurse's aide from 1959 until 1965.

Elizabeth "Libby" Fisher worked for many years, beginning in 1960, as a nursing assistant in labor and delivery. She took care of many newborn babies at the local hospital. She also worked at University Hospital in Columbus from 1950 until she returned to Lancaster in 1960.

Diane Stewart also worked for more than 25 years as a surgical nurse at the Lancaster hospital. She started her employment with the hospital in 1964 or 1965 as a surgical technician, and quickly won the respect of her peers. After her retirement from the hospital, she worked as a preschool teacher at the Berne Union Local School district.

Diane and her husband, Richard, moved to Lancaster in the early 1960s. Richard was originally from Logan but often traveled to Lancaster with his brother Bill when they were teens. Their two sisters were married and lived in Lancaster: Malva Brown, who was mentioned in an earlier chapter, and Ethel Hawkins, who worked at Wendel's Jewelers.

Richard once told me that when he and Diane were married, they had problems in Logan, so they decided to move. When they arrived in Lancaster, they could not find a house, so eventually Bertha and Rube Moss rented a house to them. The couple raised three children--Richard Jr., known as Ricky; Rodney; and Reginald, known as Reggie.

Richard led an interesting life, but he said it was not easy. He said his mother taught him to be somebody and that everyone else in his life was placed there to help him in some manner along the way. Richard served in the U.S. Army for 22 years before receiving an honorable discharge. While in the Army, he completed various military police schools, criminal investigation school, and personnel management school. He served as a Military Police for 15 years. Richard served during World War II and two tours of duty during the Korean War. The first time, he was the compound commander of a POW camp. The second tour, he was the recreation director in Korea.

Richard said he was good at putting on shows and sporting events for military personnel. The gym he ran once hosted the Korean Women's Volleyball Championship tournament that determined who went to the Olympics. He also organized the biggest boxing championship bouts in the South Pacific, with contestants coming from ships all over the area to compete in elimination bouts.

Richard received many letters of commendation, including one dated Sept. 29, 1964 from Lt. Colonel Joseph A. Mitchell. The letter read in part, "...thanks to personal sacrifices and endeavors on your part in hosting the 8th U.S. Army Company Level Softball Tournament, you established a level of accomplishment that your successors will find difficult to match. Your 'can-do' attitude was only exceeded by your 'is done' accomplishments."

After retirement from the military, Richard worked for the Ohio Youth Commission for several years at Fairfield School for Boys. In addition to other duties, he was a drill instructor. His drill team received numerous commendations for their routines and was praised by the governor of Ohio. Richard also worked at the Goodyear plant in Logan as a supervisor for eight years and as a team leader at Ralston Purina in Lancaster for eleven years.

Richard once related that his experiences have shown him that, while there may not be outright racial discrimination, standards may be set that make it difficult for blacks to reach those standards and be accepted. He once said, "I'm wary of anyone who speaks out against

Affirmative Action. Affirmative Action opens the door for a black person, but that black person has to have the ability to walk through the door."

Richard died in 2004 at the age of 79.

Shirley Saunders Jones is believed to be the first black female to be hired in the factory of Anchor Hocking Glass Corporation. Similarly, Betty Grogans and Helen Carlisle were the first blacks to work at the local unemployment office for many years. With the assistance of the Civil Rights Commission, Ray-O-Vac offered to hire their first black workers: Joe and Stanley H. Carlisle.

St. Vincent DePaul Shop, a non-profit store and food pantry to help the needy people of Lancaster showed much improvement after Bonnie Hall was named manager in 1987. She had been with the organization for almost three years prior to her appointment as manager.

Bonnie made her priority at that time for the store to get the name and location of the store out to the public and to let the community know that they accept as well as sell donations. She also established a certain level of quality, not only to the items that were sold but to make sure the store itself was clean and organized. As a result, St. Vincent is has become a busy place for people to shop and donate various items which include brand new clothes and other items.

Bonnie supervised several part-time employees and has the help of volunteers, the men of the St. Vincent DePaul Society. In addition to managing the store and setting the prices of the items, Bonnie was responsible for ordering and distributing food allotments to hundreds of people in

Fairfield County. Bonnie's sister, Sharon McGill also works at the store. Bonnie continued to manage the shop until her death in 2006.

Mike Dexter, better known to the community as "Pastor Mike," was someone who was well loved and respected by both the white and black communities. He was very active in the community and was willing to help any individual who asked to the best of his ability.

Mike was pastor of Good Shepherd Church, which was part of Maywood Mission, on the south end of town. He was employed at Anchor Hocking Corporation where he was also the chaplain. Mike loved God, first of all, his family and especially singing. After he went through some rough times in his life, and he became a born-again Christian, Mike was called by God to preach. He loved to preach. The love of God radiated from him and through him so much that it appeared most of the time that he could barely contain it. I loved to hear him preach because he gave the Word as God gave it to him. Sometimes he would be so filled with the Holy Spirit that he would run and jump and leap over the altar. Yet, he was humble, and said he was but a humble servant of God and always gave glory and honor to Jesus Christ as Lord and Savior.

The Dexter family is blessed with the gift of singing, and they have sung together as a family group since the Dexter children were young. They are often invited to other churches and local functions to sing. Their music ministry became the core of their church, and their praise and worship in song attracted people to the church and revival meetings, and have blessed many people.

Billie Jean Cunningham of Bremen said she joined Good Shepherd Church because she knew something special was taking place there.

"Pastor Mike had a way of reaching people and lifting their spirits. He had a big influence on the church. When he started as pastor, there were only three or four people attending. Now, there is an average of 100 people weekly."

Pastor Mike was loved by both the black and white community. This was evident when Mike was stricken with cancer and eventually died on April 3, 2003 at the age of 60. Several years before his death, Mike was hospitalized and was told he had a few short days to live. The hospital was overwhelmed with visitors and people who gathered there to pray. A long line of people waited just to go to the floor he was on to let his family know they were praying for Mike and for the family. The hospital staff had to tell people not to come and to allow Mike to rest. So many prayers went up, that Mike's cancer went into remission, and he was soon back into the pulpit.

When the cancer returned in 2002, Mike knew it was his time. Just days before he died, Pastor Mike was still an encouragement and blessing to those who were able to go to his house and talk with him.

Mike was able to see the fulfillment of his dream before he died. His dream was to build a church on a hill. Land had been purchased on Spring Street on the south end of Lancaster. Several people told me that a number if problems with building inspections and other roadblocks almost stopped Mike's dream of preaching in a new church.

According to Billie Jean, in March of 2003, although the church was not completely ready, the congregation set up folding chairs and held the first service in the new building on the hill.

"The congregation wanted to make Pastor Mike and Pat's 41st wedding anniversary special," Billie Jean said. "Mike made it through the service. You could see the joy in his eyes."

Jeff Graf had known Mike fro about 30 years, and saw Good Shepherd Church as a testimony to Mike's love for God and for the community.

"He was a special person, a true man of God, who was honest and had integrity. There were a few men who really show their love for God and live their life as God wants. Mike was one of these men. He showed unconditional acceptance towards everyone.

Jeff said Mike believed he was called by God to minister in the poor district in Lancaster's south end. "Mike was a light to the ones who were hurting first. He was not swayed by the ones who had money and prestige," Jeff said. "Mike was amazing. The love that he had inside him allowed him to cross different barriers to build the church into a cross-cultural, racial, and economic congregation. The love and acceptance found there is amazing."

Mike did not forget Allen Chapel. He was among the group of people to support the church during the two court battles involving Allen Chapel. When the church was reorganized, Mike helped Allen Chapel whenever possible. He and his family, or Good Shepherd Church choir took part in gospelfests and preached at revivals.

According to Mom, as head trustee, Mike was torn when he was offered pastorate at Good Shepherd Church. "Mike told me he wanted to be with Allen Chapel, but felt he was being led to go build up Good Shepherd. He made the right choice," Mom said.

Some of the black men and women had the chance to advance their careers away from Lancaster but still maintained their ties to Lancaster and the local black community.

One of the people who chose to leave Lancaster to work was Martha Belle Jackson, a 1948 Lancaster High School graduate. At LHS, Martha Belle concentrated on secretarial courses. After she graduated, she worked at Hickles in different capacities, including as an elevator operator, window decorator and stockroom clerk.

In 1963, Martha Belle took refresher secretarial courses through Manpower. It is believed that she was the first black woman from Lancaster to be hired by Diamond Power. She worked in the Industrial Engineering Department, Research and Development.

Martha Belle left Lancaster in 1969 to become executive secretary to the executive administrator of Weight Watchers of Columbus and Central Ohio. Her next upward step was when she became the secretary to State Representative Don S. Maddux of Lancaster while he headed the Ohio House Election Committee. She was also secretary to the House Judiciary Committee and the Ohio House Insurance Committee; to State Representative Harry Lehman of the 16th District, and to State Representative Mike Stinziano of the 30th District.

While working at the State House, Martha Belle received several honors. She was commended by the Ohio House of Representatives in 1981 as a leader of the '80s. She was also chosen as the Outstanding Young Woman in American Politics in 1982. She was a member of the Ohio Women and the National Women Political Caucus, the Ohio and Franklin County Democratic Party, and the American Professional Women Secretarial Institute.

Another noted citizen was Howard Ball, who graduated from Ohio State University and went on to receive his doctorate degree. At one time he was the head of the audio/visual department in the College of Education at Alabama A&M University. He retired recently and continues to live with his wife in Alabama. They are enjoying traveling throughout the world.

Jennmary (Ulmer Campbell) Boyd, a 1949 LHS graduate, received a bachelor's degree in education at Fenn College in Cleveland. She obtained a medical degree at the Ohio College of Podiatry in Cleveland in 1967. At one time, in the later years of her practice, Jennemary had a visiting practice to several nursing homes. I believe she continues to live in the Reynoldsburg area.

The three children of Tom and Malva Brown, Carol, Janet and Greg, all succeeded in their chosen professions. Carol Jones left Lancaster shortly after her graduation from LHS in 1949 and was said to have moved to Washington, D.C. She reportedly worked as a clerk at the U.S. Information Agency. She then settled in Columbus where she worked as a government quality assurance specialist at the Defense Construction Supply Center beginning in 1962.

Carol attended Central State University and later at Columbus Technical Institute (now Columbus State University) where she majored in public administration.

Janet King, a 1952 LHS graduate, left after graduation and attended Alabama A&M University. She received a bachelor's degree in Education, and worked in Alabama as a teacher.

Carol and Janet is brother, Greg Brown graduated from Lancaster High school in 1965. He was well liked by his classmates and teachers. He was class president and was a standout football athlete while in high school. Greg also attended Central State University and received his bachelor's degree in education with a concentration in Black History. He taught in the Cleveland School District and eventually received a doctorate degree in math. He later moved to Oakland, California.

Another 1965 LHS graduate, Daniel Paul Smith, the son of Emile and Olive Smith. Danny obtained his bachelor's degree in health and physical education in 1969 from Wilmington College. He taught at Buckeye Junior High School from 1969 to 1978. He was one of five teachers within the Columbus City School system to be selected as Teacher of the Year in 1978. He then taught at Independence High School, Columbus. Danny earned a master's degree in education from Xavier University. He is, at this time, dean of students at Pickerington High School North, in the northern part of Fairfield County.

Michael E. Preston worked his way through the social work field. I would say that Mike got his work ethic from his parents, Fred and Verna Preston. Fred worked for many years at the Boys Industrial School, later renamed Fairfield School for Boys. He also was a cook at Shaw's Restaurant, and both Fred and Verna worked for the Gesling family.

At one time, Mike was as associate director of personnel and staff development at North Central Mental Health Center, Columbus. Among his duties in this position was responsibility for the student internship program, which involved developing hands-on learning experience for students at Ohio State University, Columbus State Community College, Otterbein College, Capital University, and Trinity College.

Mike was chairman of the staff development committee for the Franklin County Mental health Board. This committee was responsible for advising the board of educational needs of staff members throughout Franklin County. Mike had also been active on the local, state and national levels of the National Association of Social Workers, and had been selected on three different occasions as one of 50 social workers in Ohio to participate on an interdisciplinary conference held at Ohio State University.

Teaching for Mike was not limited to students or staff members at the mental health centers. He also taught classes at the College of Social Work at OSU and conducted numerous workshops in Franklin County, Washington D.C., and Philadelphia. Mike retired in March of 2007.

Bill Stewart, a 1945 Lancaster High school graduate, worked in the social work field with troubled youth until his death in 1979 at the age of 51. Bill was an outstanding athlete in football at LHS. He was selected to play in the first North-South All-Star game in Toledo. At that time, he was the only player from Lancaster and was the only black player on the South team.

I humbly report that I was able to follow other local blacks to have worked in the social services field. I graduated from Lancaster High School in 1972 and received a bachelor's degree in social sciences from Ohio University in 1978, and completed my Master of Education degree in community counseling from the Lancaster campus of Ohio University in 1981.

I was the first black to work at the Fairfield County Mental Health Clinic (now New Horizons Counseling Center). I worked there for several years as an aftercare caseworker and was a liaison to the Central Ohio Psychiatric Hospital in Columbus. During my employment at the clinic, I participated as a member of several councils and committees and managed to be on the staff basketball team. I assisted in the development of Families In Touch, a support group for family members of mentally ill persons and lectured at several of these meetings. I later worked at Central Ohio Psychiatric Hospital through Southwest Mental Health center (now Netcare) on the admission units as an inpatient unit coordinator. After working there several years, I was seriously injured by a patient and transferred to Southeastern Correctional Institution as a unit case manager and later as a social worker in the psychological services department. I was there for ten years.

After a year as a substitute teacher, I am proud to say that I was the first black reporter to work at the *Lancaster Eagle-Gazette.* I was there for six year before I was released from my job. There are several things I could say here, but I will not. I can say that it was often a struggle while I worked there, but I sincerely hope that it was not because of racial discrimination. All things happen for a reason, however. I decided it was time to take a shot at freelancing and writing as an author. I also returned to the education field and am substitute teaching for the Lancaster City School District.

I made several attempts to break into the local political arena. In 1983, I took out petitions to run for Fifth Ward City Council seat. However, amid a little controversy, my petitions were declared invalid because several signatures were thrown out. I again ran for the same seat in 1987 against Sue Widener, a local bank administrator. I lost by a very narrow margin. I decided to try to run for the Lancaster City Schools Board of Education in 2005, which turned out to be quite interesting. Patty Moore, the president of the school board, and I took out petitions, but both were invalid. Not only did we run as write-in candidates, but two others declared their intention to run as write-in candidates. I did not win one of two seats that were open. Regrettably, there has yet to be a black person elected to a political office.

There have been a number of black students who attended Lancaster High School in the 1970s and 80s, and many were outstanding in various areas, including music or sports. As previously mentioned, Alan Saunders and Victor Jones are believed to be the first blacks to be members of the LHS Singing Gales. Victor was also well-known for his exceptional talents in both music and drama at LHS, in the community and while a student at Otterbein College. While at LHS, Victor received the Best Actor Award in 1976 and was student director in 1977. While in college, he participated in many theatrical productions. Victor was an intern with the Playhouse on the Green in Memphis, Tennessee. While there, he acted in several plays and served as assistant musical director in two other productions.

Victor was additionally selected to be an apprentice with the Kenley Players in Columbus. He was in "The Sound of Music" with Carol Lawrence, and in "My Fair Lady" with Pam Dawber. For movie buffs, Victor was in two films - as an extra in "Brubaker," starring Robert Redford, and as a zombie in "Dawn of the Dead."

Through the years, there have been black athletes who played in some type of sports while at Lancaster High School, especially football. The 1970s and 80s were no exception. The few examples cited were the ones that I was able to get information about regarding their numerous awards and recognition for their athletic abilities. It is not my intention to omit others, however.

Anthony "AJ" Saunders, a 1978 graduate, is still known for his feats on the Golden Gales football field at Fulton Field as a senior. He was known for his speed and one-handed catches. The awards he received included, the Hickles Award, WHOK Outstanding Offensive Player, All COL (Central Ohio League) Offensive Player, and was selected to the COL and District First Team. Saunders was also the first black from Lancaster to represent the South and play in the North-South All Star football game at the Hall of Fame Stadium in Canton. Ohio State University standout quarterback Art Schlichter was the quarterback for the South team at that time.

Rodney Stewart, who followed Anthony in school, also received numerous awards in football, as well as track, and played in the North-South All Star game. Both held records that were not broken until over 25 years later. Some of Rodney's records still stand.

Larry Jones was an excellent athlete in track. As a senior in 1979, Larry was 11th in the state in the high jump event. He broke the school record, previously held by Rodney Stewart, by jumping 6'6". Larry told me that he has several records that have not yet been broken.

Larry's daughter Keisha followed in his footsteps and was an outstanding athlete in track. She received a college scholarship in track and graduated from college in 2005. Larry's niece, Mandy Woodfork proved that being a standout athlete in track runs in the family. Mandy was a track star in her own right and set several records while at Lancaster High School.

While a sophomore, Mandy had an outstanding year (1989), including setting a Class AAA Southeast District record in the preliminaries of the 100-meter hurdles, with a time of 15.7 seconds. This meet took place in Lancaster on May 18, 1989. She advanced to the district is finals.

Several days later, May 21, the Lady Gales won the AAA district title, led by Mandy and teammate Tavie Burke. Mandy had qualified for the regionals in six events. Mandy won the 100-meter hurdles in a record time of 15 seconds, breaking the district mark she set in the 1988 season of 16.1 seconds. She also finished second in the 200-meter dash with a time of 25.9 seconds. She also ran on the 800-meter relay team and helped earn a berth in the regional meet.

At the regional track meet held the next week, May 28, in Mount Vernon, Ohio, the Lancaster girls' squad took fifth place. Mandy took fifth place in the 100-meter hurdles with a time of 15.89, just missing a spot to the state meet as the top four finishers in the event. Mandy's performance accounted for all of the Lady Gales' scoring.

At that same regional meet, another track star with Lancaster ties turned in a stellar performance. Stephanie Henry, then a junior at Pickerington High School, helped to lead her team to second place in the regionals. Stephanie is the niece of Stanley and Helen Carlisle of Lancaster.

Stephanie captured the individual championship in the 100-meter, with a time of 12.58 seconds; the 200-meter dash with a time of 25.89 seconds; anchored the 4x100 relay, along with Tina Starr, Laura Campbell and Chavona Price, to finish in first place; and anchored the team's 4x200 relay, along with Tina, Laura Friedlinghaus, and Janet Kushen, to second place.

Andrea "Andi" Hall, a 1983 graduate, was the first black female to be recognized for her athletic abilities. Andi received many awards and set several records as a sprinter and hurdler since she was in the eighth grade at Thomas Ewing Junior High school. Some of these awards include Most Valuable sprinter and Hurdler in 1981 and 1982, and the 1981 Southeast Sectional Hurdle Champion after she set a record of 15.4 in the 100 meter low hurdles. She was also selected in 1982 to a part of the First Team All-COL for the 400- and 800-yard relays, First Team Southeast District in the 800-meter relay and 100-meter low hurdles. She was also named to the 2nd team Southeast District in the 400-meter relay and 100-meter dash, in which she set another school record with the time of 12.8.

In addition to her excellent athleticism, Andi was an excellent student. She attended one of three vocational youth conferences sponsored by the Division of Vocational Education, State Department of Education, which was held in 1982 at Denison University. As a student at the local high school, Andi was in the clerk-typist vocational education program. She was nominated by the superintendent of the Lancaster City School District.

I would be remiss if I did not mention Tyrone "Ty" Conrad, who made an impact in the community during his short lifetime. Ty died at the age of 30 on November 16, 2001, but the spirit of who he was lives on through the establishment of a memorial fund in his name. Ty's family, friends and colleagues set up the Tyrone Conrad Memorial Fund, which is administered through the Fairfield County Foundation.

A graduate of Lancaster High School Class of 1990, Ty enjoyed boxing. He was a member of the Special Forces Boxing Club founded by his former stepfather, Kean McGill. On the night he died, Ty was one of several boxers who participated in an evening of charity boxing at AMVETS Post 1985. He fought three rounds in his match and complained of being unable to catch his breath. He passed out and died shortly after despite attempts at CPR and medics' efforts to revive him. His father, Paul Conrad, told us that they discovered Ty had a heart condition that he and his family were unaware of prior to his death.

At the time of his death, Ty worked as a probation officer for the Fairfield County Juvenile Court and at Crossroads Center for Youth, an alternative school for juvenile offenders. Doug Fisher, facility coordinator said Ty had a positive influence on the students at the youth center.

"Ty really cared for these kids and loved them. Most of the students came with nothing. Some came from abusive situations, and sometimes have no food or money with them, and Ty would hand them food or money. It was those small things that sometimes helped turn around these kids. As a Christian, Ty's spirituality always came through, and was a big part when talking to the kids. He led by example," Fisher said.

Board members for the memorial fund include James Woerner, teacher with the Lancaster City schools, Jeff Graf, with Crossroads, Rick McFarland, Doug Fisher with Crossroads, Matt Waligura, Paul Conrad, Susan "Susie" Shaw, Ty's fiancée, Debbie Beam with Lancaster City Schools, and Judge Steve Williams with Fairfield County Juvenile Court.

The memorial fund is used to help young people who have special needs. Board members included said the memorial fund is a living legacy to Ty and enables them to help him still do what he wanted to do in his life. The fund is administered in two different parts. One will provide assistance for needy children in Lancaster and Fairfield County, whether for medical assistance, such as paying for medication or treatment, an educational need, to buy clothes or shoes, or whatever is needed.

The second part of the fund is the Ty Conrad Best Behavior Award. This award is given to an elementary and a secondary school special education student who has overcome barriers and is trying to do their best in school and in the community. To be eligible, the student must be enrolled in special education classes in the Lancaster City Schools, including those who attend the alternative school at Crossroads. Each recipient receives $100.

Doug Fisher said the awards for the special education students are an appropriate part of the memorial fund. "I witnessed Ty teaching and spending time with the kids at Crossroads. He told them that having a learning disability was no excuse for not achieving successes in life. Ty set an example because he had a learning disability and still went to college and succeeded," Doug said. "Ty was strict and demanded respect from them, but he never asked them to do anything that he would not do. Ty had a great sense of humor and gave them time to relax and have fun. He showed them they could be serious and have a good time too."

Ty's family is grateful for the establishment of the fund and believes this is what Ty would have wanted. Paul said anything Ty could do to help the youth, he did. Paul said Ty believed in helping them to get a second chance in life.

Board member Debbie Beam was on of Ty's teachers at Stanbery Freshman Campus, and said the fund was a wonderful tribute to Ty.

"Ty was a good, kind, wonderful friend to everyone," Debbie said. "Even in his death, Ty still has an influence on the students. Kids have come in and said they will try harder and be successful in Ty's honor. He has and still is touching so many people in different ways."

Chapter 8

Too Black to be White;
Too White to be Black

Growing up as a minority in Lancaster has been very interesting for me. In the previous chapter, I related a few instances of discrimination towards the black residents by white citizens. But that is only one side of the coin, so to speak. The other side of the coin is just as interesting, if not surprising to the white community—that is, discrimination and being snubbed by the black community.

I have been told stories by my parents and other older adults about a screening board that was in place in Lancaster in the early 1920s until the late 1960s. This screening board consisted of black citizens and was in place to screen other blacks who tried to move into Lancaster. If they were deemed to be undesirable or had the potential to cause trouble for the black community, they were run out of town. This screening board also had a say as to who could or could not buy a house. The main focus of the screening board was to interview people from out of town and then

151

send the ones they selected to the wealthy white families whom local blacks worked for as domestic help. Only a few people really knew who was on the screening board, and it was kept hush-hushed for many years. I remember hearing about the committee when I was young and asking Mom about it. She told me I was not to talk about it. I believe it was not until the mid-1990s that people, including the white community, began to openly talk about the committee. I believe by that time, everyone on the committee had died.

It has only been in recent years that I was given several names of people rumored to be on the screening board. I was told that Josh Campbell was considered to be the black mayor of Lancaster and head of the board. Other members were rumored to have been John Westbrook, Pearl Anderson, Tom Brown, and Emile and Olive Smith. Yet, no one is still willing to talk about the particulars of the board's role in Lancaster's black community. Dad once told me that the one good thing about it was that it helped to minimize a lot of problems that other communities experienced by keeping out those who had the potential to cause trouble.

Mom recalled that she had some problems when she first came to Lancaster from Hocking County. She said before she dated Dad, she visited people with her sister and other relatives. She talked about the possibility of attending Bliss Business College and staying with a black family while going to the college. However, she decided against this and went back home.

Mom said she had mixed feelings about the people she met in Lancaster. She said a number of the black residents she met were not very friendly towards her and were somewhat condescending, mostly because she was a country girl. Even after she met and was dating Dad, she said others gossiped about her. It was not until she approached by a prominent member of Allen Chapel and of the black community and discovered they were related through Mom's father that she was accepted by other black residents.

The majority of blacks in Lancaster tend to be light-skinned, like myself and my family, because of the interracial marriages through the years. Because of my family's mixed heritage, we were taught to be proud of every one of our heritages. Mom and Dad also taught us to be more concerned with the person's character and not the skin color. But, as is true with many things, this is sometimes easier said than done.

As I have already said, the neighborhood in which I lived was racially mixed, and we have all been like family with each other. When I attended South School, there were always several other black kids in my class, and we all got along. However, my close friends were white - probably because I was the only black female in my class all through school, including high school.

Anyway, at South School, my best friends were Kathy and Karen Kilbarger, Debby Wolfinger, Melody Wachter, April Stebelton, Jill Romine, and Rosemary Robinson. We were together during and after school. I remember spending weekends and summers at the Kilbarger farm on Hamburg Road, with Debby joining us because their farm was just down the road. Likewise, the Kilbargers often stayed overnight at our house. Race was never thought of, just that we were close friends and shared many secrets, hopes and dreams, and had a lot of fun together.

My junior high school years were a little different but not really much more. I maintained friendships with my elementary school friends, while making new friends. When I entered the seventh grade, Stanbery Junior High School was transformed from the old high school to a junior high school, complete with a new wing. The black students went to Stanbery instead of Thomas Ewing Junior High. It was exciting to be a part of selecting the name, the nickname (Stanberry Defenders), school colors (brown and white), and the mascot (knight in armor on a horse). I was involved in many activities and as was the case most of the time, the only black student to participate in certain activities. It was during this time, however, that I began to experience direct prejudice.

In the previous chapters, I talked about the social discrimination, and knowing there were places where we were not supposed to go. This was an understanding on the part of the black community, and for whatever reason, we complied, and it did not bother me that much. It was something that was targeted towards the entire black community and not me personally.

Several incidents during my junior high and high school years opened my eyes to looking more closely at racial issues. I remember in the eighth grade, after gym class, we were in the locker room taking quick showers and changing our clothes before the next class. One girl wanted to borrow my spray deodorant. When I went to hand it to her, another girl said something about not using it because she might smell like a "nigger." This particular girl had been making remarks off and on, about seeing if I was built the same as white girls, and not wanting to be in the same shower with me because I was black, among other things. I had not been the direct target of unfounded hate before. I ignored her and tried to talk to her, but it did not do any good. I finally found the time when we were alone and showed her that I could hit just as hard as a white girl could, and she never bothered me again.

I realized that there were times that some of the other students were either curious or did not mean any harm. Because I am so light-skinned, some of my friends liked to compare their tans to my skin. They would put their arm up to mine and say something like "watch out Saunders, we're going to be darker than you." When we talked about boys, some of my friends tried to fix me up with a black guy. The trouble with that I was related to just about everybody. One girl tried to fix me up with a guy, someone that she thought was cute. She had no idea that this guy was my brother. Because I was very shy, she was shocked when I said I would talk to him. I went over and gave him a big hug and kiss on his cheek, and said I would love it if he would walk home with me after school. My brother did not think it was too funny at the time, but we laughed about it later.

Another incident happened to someone else but nonetheless, made me realize how people can quickly turn against a black person.

In junior high, a certain black male was very popular. He was an athletic standout, was a class officer, and was a very intelligent individual who had many white friends. However, when he showed deeper feelings for a white female student, he ran into all types of problems, and from what I understand, was basically forced to leave town.

My freshman year was the 1968-69 school year. Much had changed socially and was very complicated. The majority of my friends were the same throughout high school, but it was not as easy as it had been in the earlier school years. For awhile, I was scared to talk one-on-one to white guys who showed any interest in me, so I shied away from them unless we talked strictly about school-related matters.

I was involved with more black teens because more black families had moved into the neighborhood from bigger cities. Because of my interaction with them, I was more aware of "being black."

The McKinley family moved down the street from my family. Before the arrival of the McKinleys, while I was still in elementary school, Rev. Gordon Franklin became minister at Allen Chapel and moved his family into the church parsonage. Because of these two families, my racial horizon was broadened. We spent time at each other's houses listening to records by the Motown recording stars, such as the Temptations, Stevie Wonder, The Supremes, and others. I recall the guys would go down into the basement of our home and pretend they were The Temptations. They had the Afros, learned the dance moves and sang the best they could to the records. The McKinleys taught me the latest dance steps. They often hosted house parties on Friday and Saturday nights. We dressed up and had a lot of fun. These dances were about the only times that I spent with only black friends. It was like another world to me.

Despite these house parties, several of the McKinley girls laughed at me and told me I was "too white" to be around them. While I liked the Motown sound, I also liked to listen to The Osmonds and Simon and Garfunkel. I had a hard time doing the dances popular with the black teens.

I did not see eye to eye with some of the other black youth during the Black Movement of the late 60s and early 70s. I could not fix my hair into an Afro because the texture of my hair was too straight. I was more in favor of the peaceful changes advocated by Dr. King and not the separatism and violence if necessary teachings of Malcolm X and Stokely Carmichael. I did not know a lot of the "black slang" and was told that I talked too proper and was sounded "too white." Again and again, I was told I was "too white." There have been and still are incidents when I talk to someone on the phone, and when I meet the person face to face, he or she surprised I'm black because "I sounded white."

I recall incidents where several black teems liked to play "Selma, Alabama," talking about the senseless beating of blacks by white people during a peaceful demonstrators led by Dr. King. These black teens snatched my older brothers out of the yard, took them in the alley out of sight of our house and beat them. They liked to ride by and throw rocks and clumps of dirt at us and our white friends as we played in our backyard. Why they thought this was funny, I will never know.

I also remember a time when several black guys followed me home from school and called me a "honkey-lover" because of my white friends. Early one morning when I went to leave for school, I was frightened by a statue that was painted and left on our front porch. I cannot recall what the note said, but it pertained to being "white."

Even if some of the blacks thought I was "too white," most of the Whites did not see me as being too black. I moved in and out of their groups easily and with almost no problems. During my high school years, my family attended church at The Salvation Army. Lt. Ray Dalrymple and his wife Jan were young officers with two little boys. They were very youth-oriented and had a lot of activities for the young people, which grew in numbers while they were ministers at the Lancaster Corps. There were a number of us who did a lot of things together through the church--Joe and Brenda Alford, Rick Featheroff, Larry Anneshansley, Carolyn Bailes, Pam and Patty Courtright, and myself. Sometimes Larry's brothers, Steve and Mike joined us. We went to Columbus to see the Columbus Jets play; we went roller skating, swimming at Lake Logan; we played basketball with other Salvation Army Corps in Columbus, and we went to Van Wert, Ohio to camp on Lt. Dalrymple's parents' farm. We even went to New York City to attend a national youth conference.

We also helped out the church in different ways. We helped man the kettles at Christmas. We were in charge of the Sunrise service at Easter. We helped with the annual ham and beans supper. We taught Vacation Bible School in the summer. I organized a library at the church and was in charge of that. I was honored that summer with a presentation by the Lancaster Kiwanis Club's Church Youth Leader of the Year award.

I spent a lot of time with the Dalrymples, especially the summer of 1970. That was the summer that a girl named

Edna from Connecticut stayed with the Dalrymples. We became fast friends. That same summer, three college guys who attended The University of Nebraska stayed at the Salvation Army in the upstairs apartments until they retuned to school to start the fall term. They were Scott Petty, Jim Perry and Don Snouffer. They became a part of our group and helped us with Vacation Bible School and other activities at the church.

Most of the teens mentioned above also spent a lot of time together outside of church activities. Joe, Rick, Carolyn, Larry, Pam and I spent a lot of time together. They liked to come to my house and play and sing around the piano. We played baseball with other kids or went to the park. I remember I was sick on my 16th birthday. However, they all got together with my Mom and threw a surprise party for me.

Another group of friends and I, especially our junior and senior year, were almost inseparable. One group included Linda Brickey, Tim and Tony Nungesser, and another group Barb Hockman, Terri Russell, and Brenda Wicks. We all had so much fun together, and not once was there even a mention of race differences. They called my parents Mom and Dad and were like a part of the family. Barb and I, along with a few other school friends, including Jill Romine, Shana Rife and Sandy Jackson still meet frequently for dinner.

It was not always like that with other white teens, however. I encountered some problems of prejudice from whites while in high school. Again, although my close friends were white, however, several teachers made a part of my high school years uncomfortable, and I was unable to be involved in some activities because of being black. My biggest regret was not being able to be in Singing Gales, something I had always dreamed about being a part of because I love to sing.

I will never forget the time when I was in A Cappella Choir my junior year. We had an exceptionally good choir, and Mr. Charles Eichelberger was able to take us to several contests. We were on TV for a Christmas special, and we made a recording. We also had a choir exchange with Mentor High School, a white suburb near Cleveland.

The choir traveled to Mentor on a Friday after school and stayed all night to present a concert Saturday afternoon. We stayed with host families. We were all excited about going somewhere new and different. When we arrived at the school, we attended a reception and then paired up with the host families. When my name was called and I stepped forward, no one stepped forward. The silence was awful. I heard someone remark that they did not realize that I was black. The family finally came forward and made an excuse that something had come up and they could not take me. I was stunned and felt sick to my stomach. The person in charge went through the rest of the list. Mr. Eichelberger said he would put me up in a hotel. However, another couple approached us and said they would allow me to stay with them but cautioned that I would not be able to attend the parties that were planned for the two choirs. I accepted. It was hard sitting upstairs in the bedroom while listening to the fun downstairs. Several of my friends said they would stay with me, but I insisted they had nothing to do with what happened and to go and have fun.

Because I grew up black in a white community with an open mind, I was able to adapt easily to college life at Ohio University in Athens and get along with most anybody. At the same time, I experienced drawbacks both at OU and when I moved to Columbus after graduate school in the early 1980s.

I was able to get along with people of other cultures and races at Ohio University because of the way my parents raised me. I had friends who were white, Black Americans, Italian, African, Venezuelan, Japanese and other nationalities, and found that time to be an enjoyable learning experience. At the same time, I saw this as an opportunity to be more involved with my black peers. I attempted to join a black sorority, but was laughed at because of my fair skin. When I was asked where I lived and told them Lancaster, they laughed and said they knew I was white. I felt uncomfortable when I went to the black student union with several black friends, all who were darker than me. Since I had more problems with Ohio University's black students than whites, I slipped back into the culture I was more comfortable with, and became involved with Christian groups, including Wesley Choir and Kappa Phi, once again being the only black student in both groups.

Tina Heitmann Swearingen, a white girl from Newark became my best friend, and we shared an apartment for several years. As a voice major, Tina introduced me to opera and classical music, and "Tina beans." We remain friends and keep in touch with each other. Most of my friends were music majors and members of Wesley Choir, including David Roe and Mike McKinnis. We had a lot of fun going to concerts, football and basketball games together, as well as going on picnics, parties, dancing at our favorite club, and camping out together.

This brings back the memory of when I dated Daryl Pritchard, a white guy who played the trombone in OU's marching band. He was a wonderful person, and we had a lot of fun going to midnight movies and going uptown. I recall one time we went to a jazz spot uptown. A black guy walked up to me and loudly argued with me about being with a white guy and asked if I thought I was too good for the black guys. Before Daryl, who was getting angry, or I could say anything, I heard a female behind me tell the guy whom he was talking to that she wanted to go home. I turned and the female was white. I asked if she was with the black guy. She became somewhat defensive and said that was "her man." All I could do was look at the black guy and laugh. He knew why I was laughing and had the grace to walk away without any further words. I do not think Daryl knew quite what happened. Even though we liked each other, and his parents liked me, Daryl admitted he could not handle the pressure from his white friends for dating a black girl, no matter how light-skinned. I told him that I understood, and we remained friends until we graduated.

After graduation from OU in 1978, I returned home and worked at the Fairfield County mental health clinic. I thought that surely the profession world would be different and more tolerant and open-minded with employees, but I found out that it was not necessarily so.

Even though I had a degree and experience, I had the hand of affirmative action to help me step up to the door of opportunity to work at the local clinic. I was constantly reminded that the only reason I was there was because of affirmative action. It did not seem to matter that I worked hard, handled my caseload, volunteered for extra work and came up with fresh ideas. It did not seem to matter what I did or how hard I worked, it was never good enough. It was demoralizing and difficult for me to work under those conditions because there was no one I could talk with or who could understand my situation.

In September 1978, I went right back into graduate school at OU-Lancaster while working at the mental health clinic. Two years later received my master's degree in counseling. This even proved to be a challenge.

There were very few blacks in the program, all who were from the Columbus area. One particular professor did not seem to like me, but I dismissed it because she never directly said or did anything to me. She basically ignored me, even when I tried to talk in class. After the second quarter, she said she wondered how I got good grades (in order to stay in the graduate program, I had to get an A or a B in all my classes.) She questioned if I should be in the program. Shortly after she made that remark to me, I received a letter from Ohio University's College of Education. The letter stated that I had to meet with a panel of professors in Athens to defend my right to be in the program. No explanation was given and no account of wrong-doing was given.

I remember I was angry, humiliated, and scared at the same time. I really wanted my master's degree. Sitting in front of that panel and answering questions in details for several hours was one of the most grueling experiences in my life. I was relieved when I received a letter stating I could stay in the program.

When I went through the graduation ceremony in 1981, I saw that professor in the audience. As I walked past her I waved my diploma at her, stuck out my tongue and gave her a very uncharacteristic "birdie." I did apologize to my mother who saw me "salute" the professor. Sometimes I got tired of having to fight for what I wanted!

After I finished graduate school, I was laid off from the clinic and was the only one not to be called back to work. I even applied for my old job several months later when it was posted but was told I was not qualified for the position. So, I took a job at a mental health clinic in Columbus and eventually moved there to avoid the long commute back and forth.

Living in Columbus was a cultural shock for me. It took me back to when I was a child and Dad took us to Columbus to visit his friends. I recall my brothers and I looked at the darker-skinned people and was amazed by the color of their skin. I had never before lived among so many black people and felt completely out of place. I then understood why other blacks had said I was "too white." I remember a white woman who was more interested in dating black guys and did not really like me once told me that I might as well move back to Lancaster and leave the big city boys alone, whatever that meant. She told me that I would never be able date anyone white or black because I was too white for the black men and too black for the white men.

Even so, I made friends with several black people I worked with Edith Robinson, Wortese "TeeCee" Slappy, Eugene Chitison, and Taylor Clark. In fact, Taylor was the first black guy I dated. (Taylor died in 1999.) These friends introduced me to black society and taught me many things I missed growing up in a white community, while at the same time protecting me from the negative aspects of big city life. We often met at TeeCee's house to play dominoes or cards, to eat, watch movies, or have house parties and cookouts. TeeCee and I remain close friends and our families visit together often. I have also made contact again with Eugene and have resumed a close relationship with him.

Thanks to John and Lois Myer, and their twin sons, Ken and Karl, I was not too uncomfortable with living in Columbus. The Myers are a white family who lived in Bexley, and they were kind enough to allow me to live in their home for several years. When I talked to a friend and co-worker, Roderick "Rick" White about moving to Columbus to save driving time, he introduced me to the Myers. I stayed in their mother-in-law suite and was treated as one of the family. Ken and Karl and I became fast friends and did a lot of things together. I will always remember making Rice Krispies marshmallow treats late at night as we talked and laughed, and going to Anthony's Pizzeria for their famous stuffed pie. We maintained that close friendship after I moved into a nearby townhouse with Ken's girlfriend. I will always be grateful for their friendship, kindness, and spiritual guidance.

However, more than anything, I missed the small town environment and the friendliness and safety I enjoyed in Lancaster. I did not want to raise my daughter in Columbus and moved back to Lancaster when she was two years old.

One thing about living in Columbus that remained with me is the involvement in community events of the black community in Columbus. When I returned to Lancaster in

1987, I became involved with different civic groups and became active with Allen Chapel and the Black Interest Group. One thing that has always puzzled me is the lack of involvement by Lancaster's black community. There have been many events brought to Lancaster that should have been of interest to the local blacks, but very few attended. There are only a handful of blacks who participate in the Black Interest Group's annual banquet and who attend the annual Martin Luther King, Jr. services. A number of blacks have complained to the Black Interest Group about cases of discrimination, yet when help was provided to them to solve the problem, they backed away and never followed through to resolve the situation.

This has always been a mystery to me and others who are more involved in the community, especially given the fact that at one time, the black community was a closely-knitted community. Maybe it is because an increased number of black people moved in from other places and are not aware of or concerned with the struggles endured by the local black residents in the past, and they are simply not interested in being involved. My daughter and nieces often complain that black students who moved to Lancaster would not talk to them at school. Mom and I have encountered blacks new to town and attempted to talk to them. More often than not, they did not respond. There are so few black residents here; we want to make sure they are aware there is a sizable black community here. Mom always said, "You may not like me or want to associate with me, but at least acknowledge one another."

Another reason there may be little involvement is because there are more opportunities afforded the black residents than in the past or because race was no longer the issue it was in the past when there was overt segregation.

There have been many changes since I was a young girl. I recall when a popular black teen tried to date a white classmate. He was told that he had to leave town immediately for his own safety. It was okay to run around with whites as a group but not as a couple. However, this viewpoint changed in the late 1980s and 90s. It is common to see black-white couples, more black men and white women than white men and black women. I often laugh and say that I am surprised more when I see a black couple than when I see a mixed couple. As a result, there has been an increase in bi-racial children in the Lancaster area. A number of these bi-racial children have grown older and. more often than not, are dating or getting married to whites, and having children who look more white than black. There is nothing wrong with this. However, it is my personal concern that along with what is known among the blacks as "bleaching out" that these biracial children are not told about their black heritage and background, and that their black history will be lost to them forever.

Chapter 9

Dedication to Dolores

When writing this book, I thought for a long time what would be suitable to include as material. It dawned on me that this book would not be complete without talking about "Aunt" Dolores Carlisle. She was the driving force behind the importance of recording as much information as possible about Lancaster's black history and the people who lived here. She and I spent many long hours researching, going through old newspaper clippings, and talking to people for many years. When she died on February 5, 1999, I slacked off for awhile. I missed her so much - a lifetime of memories includes her in all areas of my life. However, I could feel her and hear her in my heart and spirit, telling me that the project was my mantle to pick up and complete. And, as always, she is right. I have felt her guiding me in many ways as I wrote this. When I thought I ran out of material to include, I found a box that her brothers gave me after she died. This box contained a wealth of information and pictures that filled in a lot of gaps. It was like she was telling me not to forget what she had collected over the years.

Dolores Carlisle was a special lady in many different ways. She was loved by the white and black communities. Knowing the obstacles she had to endure and overcome made her more special.

Born in 1933 to Wilbur and Emma Carlisle, Aunt Dolores was the second girl of a family of eight. When she was 18 months old, she was mysteriously stricken by arthritis. From that age on, Aunt Dolores was frequently in hospitals, went through at least five operations, and endured casts, braces and a lot of pain. At the age of 12 she had to use crutches to help her walk and in later years, was confined to a wheelchair.

Aunt Dolores did not allow her disabilities to handicap her. She attended public school at the 9th grade level at Lancaster High School. Her younger brother, Stanley entered the same grade the same year. Throughout the four years of high school, Stanley, who was a high school football star, carried her up and down the stairs and escorted her five minutes before and after each class period.

In high school, Aunt Dolores concentrated on clothing and art classes since dress design was her chosen vocation. She was a member of the Lancaster Chapter of Future Homemakers of America and was chosen as club historian and vice president. She also served as president from 1953-55. In April 1954, she was awarded the organization's second highest award, the State Homemakers Degree.

A 1955 Lancaster High School graduate, Aunt Dolores was in the upper third of a class of 230 students. She was a National Honor Society member and was voted by her class as the "All American Girl." She was featured in a 1955 issue of *Jet Magazine*. A picture in the magazine showed Aunt Dolores with several of her paintings. Another pictured was that of her brother Stanley carrying her to the platform to receive their diploma.

Following graduation, Aunt Dolores went through vocational rehabilitation through the Goodwill Industries and started a garment weaver business out of her home. She said she still had the dream of becoming a dress designer but did not, at that time, have the courage to live out of town to receive the necessary training. Instead, she stayed home for eight years and partially supported herself and her mother by doing garment reweaving and alterations from her home. Time proved that she did not have enough knowledge and confidence to render the necessary service to her customers and to be able to earn complete financial support. So, Aunt Dolores again applied to the state Bureau of Vocational Rehabilitation for additional training in dressmaking and tailoring. She said she was ready to make the move because she was given a new gift, the gift of Faith. She said with Faith, she was willing to trust God and to go wherever the training was available.

In 1963, Aunt Dolores went to Cleveland to Mrs. Amanda Wicker's school for her training. In April 1965 she completed her schooling and graduated from the Clarke School of Dressmaking and Designing. Following graduation, she applied for and received a scholarship to receive additional training in tailoring, drafting and alterations of men's clothing as an apprentice to a competent tailor.

Aunt Dolores operated her shop from her home and rendered services in all the areas that she had learned. She had many loyal customers, most of who came because they heard of her excellent reputation. I, along with her customers, used to marvel at her magic in sewing and reweaving. In addition to her sewing business, Aunt Dolores operated a shop which was part of the Heartwarmer Group. She sold items aimed at people who were ill or in need of cheering up. She designed and made some of the items. Most of the proceeds from this corner shop were given back to the hospital organization. She ran her business and shop until 1993 when her declining health made it difficult to maintain.

Aunt Dolores was very active at Allen Chapel AME Church until she withdrew with others in the early 1960s. As a small child, I remember she played piano for church. She and Mom worked with the children for the Easter, Christmas, Mother's Day and Father's Day programs. I looked for her encouraging nod and proud smile as I recited my lines or sang the songs we learned.

When the small group withdrew from Allen Chapel and formed Grace Baptist Church, Sunday morning services were eventually moved from my parents' home to Aunt Dolores' home. I was one of a handful of kids in her Sunday school class. We met in her small bedroom, huddled around her bed. Aunt Dolores told us Bible stories and how to relate them to our own lives. She drilled us on the books of the Bible and stressed the usefulness of memorizing Biblical Scriptures. She conducted "sword drills" with us, where she would call out a Bible verse, and the first one to find it stood and read it. The drill was that she would say "Attention," and we sat straight in our seats. She then said "Present arms," and we placed our Bible on our right shoulder. She then read the verse we had to find and then said "Ready, fire." When the pastor conducted sword drills for the entire church, members of our class won the most times.

Aunt Dolores loved music and playing the piano. She taught me to play when I was about 9 or 10 years old, just before she left to go to school in Cleveland. She made flash cards of musical notes, scales and symbols and to teach me how to read music. She said if I could read music and knew where the notes are on the keyboard, then I could play anything. I did not get very far in the book before she left, but she said she expected me to play a song from the hymnal when she returned. I thought she was ready to burst with pride when I got up in church and played "Wonderful Words of Life."'

I cannot mention Aunt Dolores without talking about her mother, Emma Carlisle, better known by everyone as Aunt Emmie. She loved children and expressed this love in many simplistic ways.

As a child growing up in the 1960s, many of my childhood memories are tied to their home at 547 E. Walnut Street. Aunt Emmie and Aunt Dolores kept quite busy all year round. In the summer, they kept homemade popsicles in the freezer. I remember my brothers and our friends often stopped in to enjoy one or two popsicles after a long hot afternoon of play at Elmwood Park. In the winter, they warmed us up with hot cocoa and toast. At Christmas, Aunt Emmie spent many weeks baking cookies. She used to decorate shoeboxes for the children and filled them with homemade cookies. Halloween was the time when children looked forward to the most, when Aunt Emmie made her famous popcorn balls. No one I know of before or since could make better popcorn balls. Everyone headed for Aunt Emmie's house first before they were gone. Kids lined up for about half a block as early as possible. My brothers and I, our close friends, and other cousins enjoyed walking by the other kids in line to go straight into the house to get ours.

On many Friday nights, Aunt Emmie organized slumber parties for children of different ages. She always had organized games, stories and good food. Anther big event was the yearly birthday party she held for family members in August. She had a different theme every year and either made or had Aunt Dolores help her make presents connected to the particular theme. Each child received the gifts. I still have my stick horse that was made when I was 5 or 6 years old.

It was obvious to everyone who came in contact with Aunt Emmie that her love for people flowed from her love for God. She corrected us many times by simply saying, "Do you think Jesus would like for you to do that?" She read Bible stories to us and instilled in us a deep faith in God. She was behind the Saturday afternoon Bible clubs held at her home: God's Army for older boys, Mary and Martha Club for older girls and Sunbeams for the younger girls.

I was a part of the Mary and Martha Club. Aunt Emmie and Aunt Dolores taught us girls the importance of listening to God's Word as Mary did and being of service to others as Martha did. We learned arts and crafts, basic sewing and cooking; how to bake simple things; how to set a table, manners, and how to get along with others, all which tied in with the teachings of Jesus. We also played games. Our favorite was the Nabisco Cookie Game, a board game used with Nabisco cookies because we got to keep the cookies we won for our snack. We could not run up the street to Bay's Market fast enough when she asked us to get a pack of variety cookies for the game.

Aunt Emmie died in 1967 when I was in the sixth grade. I remember the funeral was well attended. Afterward, we gathered as a family for food. We ended up playing softball, making it seem more like a family picnic than a funeral. However, this was fitting for Aunt Emmie, who always enjoyed it when the family gathered and had fun together. She herself provided many pleasant memories for many people, black and white, of all ages through the years.

Aunt Dolores went on to become one of most community-minded black residents. She was a member of the board of directors for the Center for Disabilities and Cerebral Palsy. She was the president of the board for the Center for Disabilities before the organization merged with the Cerebral Palsy Center. The board arranged transportation for disabled people and provided them with the equipment they needed to complete their daily duties. In addition, Aunt Dolores was part of the executive committee and a member-at-large with the local Community Action Agency.

When I became an adult, Aunt Dolores became more of a friend, a confidante and religious advisor. I used to prop myself up on her wooden stool, and we talked and laughed about many things. She loved God with all her being, and this reflected in everything she did. She was also proud to be a black woman. We shared concerns about being black in Lancaster, the problems we faced and what we could do to solve them. Aunt Dolores was a charter member of the Black Interest Group. We moved our meetings to her home for her convenience. She had a wealth of knowledge about the past history of blacks in the community. She conveyed the importance of recording this information so that the future generations knew that we were, indeed, a part of the history of Lancaster.

Aunt Dolores loved life and lived it to the fullest of her physical capabilities. She was at all the family reunions and family gatherings. She even went to the swimming pool, watching and laughing, and tried to sound stern when we splashed her or shook off the water onto her. She supported the reorganization of Allen chapel and attended special programs even though she remained active at Grace Baptist. She was involved in many other things, especially championing those issues that concerned the physically disabled. Wherever she went, with the assistance of her trained helping dog, Clancey, she was surrounded by the people who loved and admired her.

To those who knew her, Aunt Dolores was a brave lady. She endured much pain and many operations. From 1972 to 1980, the arthritic condition took a different form, the erosion of the bones. She had to undergo six major surgeries during this time period: two hip joint replacements, one revision, and two operations on her right hand and one to stabilize her neck vertebra. Yet she seldom showed the pain or the fear she must have felt at times. When I asked her how she felt, she would say a few words and then asked how I was and what was new with me. Shortly before her death, Aunt Dolores was confined to her bed. When she died, I imagined her surrounded by her mother and other family members, laughing and trying out her new legs, arms and hands. Although I still miss her, my soul rejoices that she is where she had the faith all of her life to be--a place where there is no sorrow or sickness, a place where God dwells, reunited with her family and friends who also accepted Jesus as Lord and Savior.

I recall as little kids, we used to measure ourselves against Aunt Dolores and were tickled when we became taller - which did not take long since she was a short lady. But I knew that I would not be able to out-measure the way she was able to be a living witness for God and how she touched so many different lives in so many different ways. No one person could be around Aunt Dolores and not be aware of God's mercies and love because she radiated this. Her spirit transcended her physical limitations. I will always remember the things that she taught me and will continue the work that we started. I know that she is watching me from heaven with the same encouraging nod and proud smile.

Chapter 10

My Family

As I reflect on my past at this stage of my life, I feel blessed that I grew up here in Lancaster. Good or bad, right or wrong, everyone who was in my life, every experience I had, had some type of impact on my life and helped to shape me to be the person I am today.

My parents were disciplinarians and applied the same rules to all who played at our house, white or black. As a testament to Mom and Dad, these same kids periodically return as adults, sometimes bringing their children and recalling the "glory days." They often laugh about what Mom and Dad did when they broke the rules and about how we stopped playing in mid-stride to run home when we heard Dad whistled. By the same token, most of the homes I went to as a child also had house rules that I followed or risked punishment by the parents of that home and then by my own parents when I got home.

It is not possible in this book to include all the memories that I have recalled while writing, some things I had not thought of for years, but I thought something would be lacking if I did not sketch a few for you.

As a little girl and through my elementary school days, the years were filled with good memories. Kenny played peewee football at Cherry Street Park. I liked to go with him to practice. They made me the team's mascot, and the next year, a junior cheerleader. I was also a cheerleader at South School during fourth, fifth and sixth grades. I recall the long hours playing with the neighborhood gang – playing baseball or kickball in the alley between the feed mill and the junkyard or in our backyard. We played tag, Mother-May-I, and other games we made up for fun. After a good rain, we looked for night crawlers, whether to sell for bait or to use for ourselves to fish at Silver Lake (now Cenci Lake). We used to collect glass pop bottles, and Roger at the mill bought them from us so we could buy penny candy at Bay's Market located at the corner of Walnut and Maple streets.

I remember walking down the tracks to play with my cousin, Wendy Keels. She had Barbie dolls and made clothes for them. I did not care that much for dolls, but it was nice spending time with her.

Kenny and Jimmy King were interested in model rockets and sent off for kits. They launched them by using a small transformer. Neighbors came and watched when they held their launchings.

We also liked to sit out late at night, look at the stars with telescopes. We sometimes talked about what we thought our lives might be when we became adults but then thought how far off that was to worry about at that time.

When I reached junior high school, I still liked to play sports and hanging out with different friends, I also became more involved with community activities.

During my early teen years, Joan Carlisle and Ida Hawkins started a 4-H group, and I was asked to be their junior 4-H leader. This group was for the younger girls, who included Verna Nichols, Bonita "Bunny" Carlisle, Robin Jones, and Connie Jo Smeltzer. We introduced them to simple cooking and sewing.

Sometime later, Mom and Bonnie Hall organized a 4-H group for the younger neighborhood kids. The group included my younger siblings, Alan, Anthony, Kevin, and Valeria; Christy and Lori Hall, and Victor Jones. They formed a drill team. I also was on the team to even out the number. We practiced marching up and down Locust Street under Bonnie's orders and choreography. We marched in the 4th of July parade one year. Mom, Bonnie, and the little ones, including my youngest brother, Evan, were in the back of a car with the boom box taking care of the music. We received a lot of applause and cheers along the route.

High school was the years of attending football and basketball games, dances and parties. On weekends, Terri Russell, Brenda Wicks, and I liked to run around town in Terri's 3-wheeled "Flippo" car – it ran on a lawn mower engine, and the front end of the car was the only door. We cruised Memorial Drive, and in and out of Frisch's and Kenny's Drive-In with everyone else who wanted to see and be seen--a popular pastime during the late 1960s and early 70s.

Despite the good times I had and the acceptance I enjoyed among my white friends, I realized what was the most important was the people who had the most influence on my life, especially family.

I have already mentioned the black people who lived on Locust Street, but not what they meant to me. I spent a lot of time at Malva Brown's home, especially when her granddaughters, Vicky and Sheila Jones visited her. I also remember how she was there whenever Mom and Dad needed her. I was only 4 years old when my brother, Robert "Bobby" died at the age of 2 years. Malva came over and helped Mom, then took Kenny and me to her house when the ambulance arrived to take away his body. Lawrence was too sick to leave the house. There was a special connection with Malva – her brother Frank Stewart was married to my mom's sister, Mabel Evans Stewart, so she was family. I remember when she began to suffer from the effects of Alzheimer's. For whatever reason, one of the few things she could remember was my parents' names and phone number.

Bonnie Hall looked out after the neighborhood kids as well. Her children were more the ages of my younger siblings. Bonnie had spaghetti dinners and dances in her home for that age group. When Evan was younger and always riding his bike, he was hit by a car in front of her house. Bonnie was right there to make sure he was okay. Another time, I was riding my bike down the street, I somehow crashed my bike and flew over the handlebars. I landed hard on my back and knocked the wind out of me. Bonnie was the first person I saw. She calmed me down and helped me to breathe normal again. I was glad she was there. I always enjoyed talking to Bonnie because she always had an opinion and was not shy about sharing it.

I recall walking past where her father, Noah Carlisle lived, on Locust Street on the other side of Maple Street. Whenever he was out on the porch or in the yard, I waved to him and chatted briefly.

I always passed the home of Verna and Fred Preston, who lived on Walnut Street. Fred was a little gruff, and I was somewhat wary of him as a little girl. But I always stopped and said hi and enjoyed talking to Verna. After Fred passed away, Verna became closer to our family. She has been very supportive of what we do, especially what our children are involved with at school. She went to band concerts, choir concerts, plays, and just about any event we attended. She has a wonderful sense of humor and is fun to visit. She walks everywhere and, being in her 80s, calls herself "an old tough turkey bird."

The home of Sam and Mary Nichols on Wheeling Street was another frequent stop for me. Sammy, Jr. and I are the same age and were in the same class most of the time. I liked to spend time with his little sister, Verna. When I went to college in Athens, Verna often rode the bus down to Athens on Friday to spend the weekend with me and went back on Sunday.

Sam worked hard for his family. I always remember him with a smile on his face, but I knew he could be stern when necessary. Mary was like my mom. In fact, they looked a lot alike, and people often mistook one for the other. I remember times when Mom took me to Mary's house so she could "press" my hair. This involved heating a hot comb on the stove, putting grease on sections of my hair, and straightening out my hair. When she finished, she rolled my hair in curlers to give my hair nice curls. This gave Mom and Mary a chance to "catch up" on news. They both were actively involved at Allen Chapel A.M.E. Church. Mary was well known for her cooking, especially sweet potato pie.

Rosalie Booker and Dolly Scott lived across the street from the Nichols. They were two of my favorite older people. Rosalie was quiet and soft-mannered, while Dolly was more opinionated and loved to laugh deeply. I sat for hours listening to their stories and advice about life. Rosalie and I shared the same birthday. I made a point when I was older to take her a rose and/or a card or sometimes a piece of cake to share with her. After Dolly died, Rosalie spent time at the adult daycare at the Salvation Army, where she was adored by people of all ages. She was 100 years old when she died.

Bill and Frances "Sis" McKinley lived a little ways down the street, across from Maple Street United Methodist Church. Bill was the brother of Walter McKinley who lived down the street from us. I often waved to them, and if they had time, chatted for a few minutes.

Mulberry Street was where a number of black families also lived. Aunt Shirley Jones. who is Dad's sister; Phyllis Hawkins; Joan and Wilbur Carlisle, who was Dad's first cousin; Libby Fisher; Grant and Betty Grogans; and Mike and Pat Dexter made their homes there.

I remember Wilbur and Joan hosted a lot of family get-togethers. I recall many Friday or Saturday nights were spent there to eat homemade pizza. The men played cards or horseshoes; the women talked and were in the kitchen cooking or cleaning, and the kids played in or outside. Wilbur had a big barbecue pit in the backyard, so the family often went there for cookouts.

I appreciated Joan, especially as an adult. We both worked for the Department of Rehabilitation and Corrections, but at different prisons. We spent a lot of time talking about our problems and situations, which was hard for others to understand. Joan was very light-skinned but was very vocal about being black and outspoken about racial discrimination. She did not hesitate in speaking out against racial injustice and was right there for the young people whenever we had problems.

I remember spending a lot of time with my aunts, uncles and cousins. When I was younger, we used to go to the Hawkins farm on Rainbow Drive for picnics and family reunions. For whatever reason, the reunions gradually dropped off until we started them back up for one of Dad's birthday party. Since then, every August, we hold the annual Hooper-Hawkins reunion, which is a three-day event. We meet and greet on Friday night with refreshments, games, and karaoke, since we are a family who love to sing. The big picnic is held on Saturday and ends on Sunday with a church service and luncheon.

Anyone who came to one of our reunions would truly find out what Jesse Jackson meant about a Rainbow Coalition. Our family consists of every color of the black race – from very light to very dark. Members of the family are also white, Hispanic, and Filipino, and other nationalities.

The roots of the Hooper-Hawkins family tree can be traced back to George and Emma (Hooper) Hawkins. According to my dad, Emma Woods was born in Circleville in May 1870 to James Woods, and unknown mother. She became pregnant at a young age and was sent to what was known as the Old Folks Home located on Granville Pike (State Route 37), now known as the Clarence E. Miller County Administrative Building. While a resident there, she somehow met James Hooper, who owned his own home in the Lancaster area. He did not have a family of his own. He married Emma, who gave birth to Ida. Emma and James also had several children, Ella, Bill, Sadie, and Charles "Charlie" Hooper.

James, who was much older than Emma, died. Emma eventually met and married George Alonzo "Lon" Hawkins, who was born in November 1872 to Joseph and Harriet Gray. The couple had five daughters, Mamie, Theodosia "Dodie," Harriet "Hattie," Emma, and Minnie.

While we honor all of our past family members, during the reunion we pay special tribute to the three sisters who represent the different branches of our family tree – Minnie Saunders, Emma Carlisle, and Theodosia "Dodie" Byrd.

Minnie was Dad's mother, my grandmother. Grandma had my dad with Richard Hunster, who died in his early 20s in a drowning accident at Buckeye Lake. As I have already stated, my dad, Kenneth Eugene married Alice Mae Evans from Hocking County. Their children are Kenneth Eugene, Jr., Lawrence Richard, Hollie Ann, Robert Alonzo (deceased),

Alan Keith, Anthony Jay, Kevin Wayne, Valeria Irene, and Evan Scott.

Grandma met and married Floyd "Happy" Saunders, who was from the Nelsonville area. They had three children, James, George, and Shirley.

Grandma lived up the street from us, at the corner of Locust and Sycamore streets. She babysat us on occasions and cooked for us when Mom was in the hospital (I loved her apple and cherry pies!). I remember we went up to her house on Christmas to get presents after we opened our presents at home and ate breakfast. When she moved over on Walnut Street, I walked past her house on the way home from classes at Ohio University-Lancaster. She seemed to know my schedule. She at a table by her dining room window and held up a pot of tea. I stopped in and shared tea and cookies with her and talked about what I was doing and whatever else came to mind.

Grandma's daughter, Aunt Shirley was married for awhile to Maurice Jones, and had five children, Robin, James "Brubby," Larry "Sticks," Mary Frances, Jonathon "Johnny," and Jared. After Aunt Shirley's divorce, she and the kids lived briefly on Lawrence Street. They all used to come up to the house to play with my younger brothers and sister, especially Larry. They later moved to Mulberry Street. Aunt Shirley is now married to a Baptist minister, Robert Hunter, and lives in Pataskala.

Uncle Jim lived with Grandma. He was a fantastic cook, artist, and collector of antiques and fine furniture. He was also a wonderful gardener – I liked to tease him about stealing green tomatoes from his garden, and he always jokingly threatened me. My favorite memory of Uncle Jim was when he invited the family for a special garden dinner. He required us to dress up for the occasion. He set up a table outside, which was formally and elegantly set and decorated. He had lanterns placed around the garden, and soft classical music playing on the record player. Uncle Jim served a five-course dinner that he had prepared. It was very lovely, and I felt very grown-up.

Uncle Jim worked for awhile at Grilli's restaurant and pizzeria. I remember sometimes on Friday nights, Uncle Jim fixed a pizza for us and brought it to us when he got off from work. He also worked at the Lancaster Country Club. He worked for many years as a meat cutter at Big Bear East until his sudden and unexpected death in the early 1990s.

Uncle George was more like a big brother than an uncle. He was still in school when we were born. He was Vice-president of his junior class and played on the high school football team. Uncle George often came down to watch us or to play with us when Mom needed an extra hand. He tossed the football with Kenny and Lawrence. I remember we called him "Uncle Butterfingers" when he dropped the ball. Uncle George was the one who taught me how to play hopscotch, jacks, and seven-up. We spent hours on the front porch playing jacks when I was younger.

Uncle George had nicknames for us. He called me "Ragg-Mopp Annie" and shortened it to "Moppy Annie." I remember one year he took Kenny, Lawrence and me out for trick-or-treat night. He helped me with my costume. He bought a new mop head and put it on me like a wig. He painted my cheeks with red dots and put lipstick on me. When people asked me if I was Raggedy Annie, Uncle George laughed and said no, I was "Moppy Annie."

I was still in elementary school when Uncle George went into the Navy. I remember I was upset because he left, but Mom helped me, as well as Kenny and Lawrence, to write letters to him. I just could not convince him, though, to bring me back a bagpipe when he said he was going to be at port in Scotland.

Upon discharge, Uncle George met and married Aunt Jackie, who was from Circleville. They eventually moved to Columbus. They have two children, Glenn and Cassandra.

Emma Carlisle or Aunt Emmie represented the head of the Carlisle-Keels clan. I have already talked about Aunt Emmie. She was married to Wilbur "Teet" Carlisle. Their children include Charles, Wilbur, Stanley, Joseph "Joe," Gladys, and Dolores.

Charles was very close to Dad, as friends as well as cousins. Dad said Charles had a twin brother, George, who died as an infant.

Wilbur married Joan and had Steve, Bruce, Bonita "Bunny," Linda, Penny, and Tracy Carlisle.

Stanley married Helen and had Eric and Danielle.

Joe was married to Beverly, divorced and is now married to Karen. Joe's children are Joe, Jr., Mary Margaret, Norma Jean, Kathy, and Melanie.

Gladys married Frank Keels and had Frank, Jr., Wendy, Pat, Andy, Jeff, Judy, and Emma Jean.

Dolores was never married.

Aunt Dodie was part of the Akron branch of the family. Her children were Betty Jane, Edmund, Carl, and Leon. I loved it when she came down to visit. She loved to give big hugs and asked where her sugar was--what she called kisses. There was no getting away from those hugs and kisses. She was a gentle soul, deeply religious, and seldom had a harsh word to say. When Aunt Dodie, Grandma, Dad, and his cousins, Bobbie and Wanda got together, they talked, told stories, and laughed a lot. Just hearing them laugh until they cried made everyone else laugh.

I remember Dad took us to Akron several times to visit Aunt Dodie and different family members. I liked to stay with Aunt Annistene. She had good stories to tell. She talked about the days when she performed with jazz legends, including Count Basie, Duke Ellington, Lionel Hampton, and Ella Fitzgerald.

I'm glad that the Akron branch of the Hooper-Hawkins family has decided to maintain contact with the family here in Lancaster and have attended the family reunion. Even though most of them have not lived in Lancaster, this is still their home.

Looking back at those family members who have passed on and the ones who are left, I can say that we are blessed because we have always been taught two important factors in life--family and God. Both of these, as well as being respectful to all people, regardless of race and color, are central to who I am and what is important to me. I hope and pray that others can come to realize this as well and to learn to appreciate their own family and heritage.

In Closing...

This book has been a journey for me in many ways. It started out as a way to talk with people about the past and to help Aunt Dolores gather information and label pictures of people before anyone forgot who they are and how they fit into the family. Along the way, we realized that talking about the past and gathering information did not do anything unless we put it in a book format. We realized that our history is deeply entwined into the history of white Lancaster and that our stories and our accomplishments are just as important to the growth and vitality of Lancaster as the Ewings, the Shermans, and other famous citizens. We also realized that while the population of blacks in Lancaster has always been small in number, our contributions to our community have been many. As such, we think that people outside our community can identify with our story and that they can get some inspiration or even identify with what it is like to be black growing up in a white society while being proud of their black heritage.

It is with faith, hope and determination that our local black history can now be preserved in the history of Lancaster and not just be talked about during Black History Month in February.

Black History Month was set aside so there would be dialogue about the accomplishments of black Americans. During February, schools talk about famous black scientists and inventors; newspapers print articles about blacks and racism, and television is inundated with programming and movies that feature black performers and actors.

In January, the Martin Luther King, Jr. holiday is celebrated to reflect on what King accomplished during the Civil Rights era. At the end of February, it is then time to put everything back on the shelf until next January and February, and everyone can feel good and say they did their duty by observing Black History Month. Now they can relax until next year. Or can they? Should they?

I think it is great that one month is set aside for people to learn about black Americans and their contributions to society. People need to realize that if it were not for blacks, we would not have things we take for granted, such as traffic lights, blood transfusions, and peanut butter. Sadly, the fact remains that there is a need for a time to remember these things.

Blacks have been in this country since the first white settlers arrived here in the 1600s. However, when the land had to be cleared to raise crops, the black population was forced to do the work as slaves. There seemed to be an endless supply from various countries. As such, blacks were the only race of people who came to this country involuntarily. They were denied the right of citizenship in a country that they were forced to develop. Slavery, thus, became a dark scourge in the history of America. Many people died on packed slave boats during the Middle Passage from Africa to the West. They were branded, inspected and sold in the same manner as horses, cows and other animals. Families were split apart. They were badly abused, beaten, and even killed for trying to hold on to their human dignity.

President Abraham Lincoln delivered the Emancipation Proclamation in 1864 and "freed" the slaves from physical bondage. However, freedom remained more of a concept than reality.

The Reconstruction Era that followed the Civil War brought about the birth of the Klu Klux Klan. The KKK proclaimed their reign of terror to be ordained by God, and, senselessly and without remorse, maimed, lynched, and killed hundreds of thousands of blacks for the simple reason that their skin was dark. White sympathizers and abolitionists were also terrorized and killed for helping the blacks. This continued until the dawn of the Civil Rights Movement in 1954.

It was not until the Civil Rights Bill of 1963, enacted by President Lyndon Johnson, that Black Americans, especially in the South, were viewed as full citizens of the United States. However, this did not stop the KKK, racists, and other white supremacy groups from beating, killing, and imprisoning them. These white groups thought they could silence the voice of nonviolence, peaceful integration, and equality for all by assassinating leaders, such as Martin Luther King, Jr., Medgar Evers, and the three freedom riders from "up North" who went South to help register blacks to vote.

Thank God that these white groups did not succeed. For every one voice that was silenced, there were a hundred more to cry out against the injustice.

We are now into the new millennium. All I have said took place as early as 400 years ago and up to 30 years ago - all history and recorded in many places. Things should be different. But it is not different for black Americans, even in 2007. I am still constantly outraged and confused by the injustice and discrimination that our race must endure. It is something that we wake up with and fall to sleep with every day of our lives. There has been a resurgence of the KKK and various factions of white supremacist groups in the past several years. It was not that long ago when someone drew a Nazi sign and racial epithets on my office window when I worked at Southeastern Correctional Institution. I was simply told to wash it off. Shamefully, nothing more was done.

Today's black youth are more advantaged, but they are uneducated about the sacrifices made by those who came before them. I was shocked when a black teen, when asked, told me that Martin Luther King, Jr. was "some guy who had a dream about something but was shot."

Churches and other social organizations have become complacent and tend to give "lip service" only when it comes to equal rights. They have forgotten that the churches and pastors were in the forefront and were leaders in the struggle for civil rights.

In 1999, I remember watching the news on television as well as reading in the paper an incident that involved a black man in a small Texas town of Jasper. James Boyd, Jr. was walking home after a party and encountered three young white men who offered him a ride home. Instead, without cause, they chained him, hooked him to the back of their truck, and literally dragged him to death. John William King, one of the three men, was found guilty and was sentenced to die. Yet, he showed no remorse whatsoever and had so much hate inside him that he smirked and cursed Byrd's family. After all, he said he wanted to start his own white supremacist group and thought by killing Byrd he would bring in recruits. This was one of the worst racial crimes noted since the Civil Rights era. Yet it did not stop a radio announcer from saying on the air that it was people like singer Lauryn Hill who made white people want to drag blacks through the streets.

If anything came from Byrd's senseless death, maybe it shocked and outraged people of all races. Maybe it woke people out of their slumber and helped them to realize that we are all one people with different physical traits, characteristics and backgrounds, but, nonetheless, human beings. God is not a respecter of persons, and, as His creations, neither should we. Maybe people will realize that the history of Black Americans has been written with blood and tears of despair and bottomless sorrow.

Yet, it has also been written with determination, faith and hope, all which have allowed us to endure. Maybe this is what should be told in February instead of talking about familiar people, such as Martin Luther King, Rosa Parks, and Harriet Tubman over and over again. Maybe people will realize that it is not just black history but American history. If our story is told as American history, then maybe people will realize that we all have a responsibility towards each other as fellow Americans and must stop the senseless racism before it destroys us all.

Time has a way of fading memories from the minds of people, but, hopefully not from our hearts. It is my hope that this book will help people remember and thus be proud of what our forefathers accomplished, no matter how small, and then build onto that as our legacy to our future generations.

Emma Woods
Hooper Hawkins

George Alonzo Hawkins

Aunt Delores Carlisle

Cecilia Cameron,1897
at approximately age 25

Allen Chapel A.M.E. Church and parsonage

"The Neighborhood Gang"

Scipio Smith
First preacher at Allen
Chapel A.M.E. Church

Golden Gloves Champions
Wilbur and Charles Carlisle

The Hunster Brothers and their band

"Say and Do Club"
auxiliary of Allen
Chapel

Saunders Family Portrait

References

Allen Chapel A.M.E. Church roster, not dated

Allen Chapel A.M.E. Church Fortnightly Club minutes, November 13, 1960.

Barnes, Dwight, *Lancaster Eagle-Gazette*, February 28, 1996, n.p.

Fisher, Chuck, *Lancaster Eagle-Gazette*, February 18, 1984, n.p.

Lancaster Eagle-Gazette, December 13, 1897, n.p.

Lancaster Eagle-Gazette, "Lancaster Happenings," October 25, 1962, n.p.

Saunders, Hollie, Allen Chapel, A Brief History

Allen Chapel was long part of Lancaster, *Lancaster Eagle-Gazette*, March 12, 1991. p.6.

The Arrival of Blacks in Lancaster, *Lancaster Eagle-Gazette*

Earliest Residents' Children Carried on Traditions, *Lancaster Eagle-Gazette*, February 11, 1983, p.9.

Early Citizens Successful in Business, *Lancaster Eagle-Gazette*, March 30, 1993.

Our Black citizens, Past and Present, *Lancaster Eagle-Gazette*, March 2, 1983, p.6.

Turner, Herbert M., *Fairfield County Remembered: The Early Years*. Athens, OH: Ohio University Press, 1999.

Watts, Deward, *200 Years of Lancaster Black History, A Walk through Time*, February 26, 2005. Character Profile for Historical Reenactment, n.p.

Personal interviews taken over a period of time of the following individuals:

Azbell, Minnie

Barnes, Dwight

Beam, Debbie

Carlisle, Dolores

Carlisle, Joan

Carlisle, Steve

Cunningham, Billie Jean

Conrad, Paul

Fisher, Doug

Graf, Jeff

Grogans, Betty

Hazelton, Virginia

Kelley, John

Morrow, Alice

Rockwood, Debbie

Saunders, Alan

Saunders, Alice

Saunders, Kenneth Sr.

Smith, Danny

Stewart, Richard

CPSIA information can be obtained
at www.ICGtesting.com
Printed in the USA
BVHW081147050720
582986BV00002B/174